LUIS DE CAMÕES
Epic & Lyric

Translations by KEITH BOSLEY · *Illustrations by* LIMA DE FREITAS

With essays by Maurice Bowra, Helder Macedo and Luis de Sousa Rebelo,
and with engravings by Blake, Fragonard and others

Edited by L. C. TAYLOR

In association with The CALOUSTE GULBENKIAN FOUNDATION

First published in Great Britain in 1990
by CARCANET PRESS LIMITED
208-212 Corn Exchange Buildings
Manchester M4 3BQ

This book is part of a series *Aspects of Portugal* published in Great
Britain by Carcanet Press in association with the Calouste
Gulbenkian Foundation and with the collaboration of the Anglo-
Portuguese Foundation.

SERIES EDITORS: Eugenio Lisboa, Michael Schmidt, L. C. Taylor

British Library Cataloguing in Publication Data

Camões, Luis de, 1524-1580
    Epic and Lyric
    1. Title
    869.1'2

ISBN 0-85135-832-0 cased
ISBN 0-85135-835-5 paperback

Typeset by Paragon Photoset, Aylesbury
Printed and bound by SRP Ltd., Exeter

Acknowledgements

The essay by Sir Maurice Bowra is an abbreviation of the chapter on
'Camões and the Epic in Portugal' in *Virgil to Milton* and appears by
permission of the estate of C. M. Bowra.

The poem by Roy Campbell 'To Camões' is taken from his book
Portugal and appears with permission from Francisco Campbell
Custódio and A. D. Donker (Pty) Ltd.

The cover, lettering apart, reproduces a painting by Lima de Freitas.
His black-and-white illustrations appearing here have been
selected and adapted from editions of Camões published by Artes,
Lisbon (1957) and Circulo de Leitores, Lisbon (1972/73).

The engravings on page 98, and the photographs by Luis Filipe
Oliveira on pages 101 and 105 are from the Arquivo de Arte – Centro
de Documentação e Pesquisa of the Calouste Gulbenkian Foundation,
Lisbon and appear with permission. The editor wishes to thank Dr.
Maria Emilia Oliveira Machado for her suggestions and her help.

The engravings by Fragonard and Desenne originally appeared in
an edition of Camões published in Paris in 1817. They were issued
in a portfolio by the Ministry of Culture in Lisbon in 1972. The
editor wishes to thank Dr. Maria de Lourdes Simoes de Carvalho at
that Ministry for her suggestions and help.

The engraving by Blake on page 94 came from the City Art Gallery,
Manchester and appears with permission.

The engraving on p. 99 and the photographs on p. 102 are part of the
archives of the Diário de Notícias, Lisbon and appear with permis-
sion.

The photograph by Nicholas Sapieha on page 103, and that by Serge
Culbenkian on page 102 were specially taken for this publication.
The editor wishes to thank the photographers for their help.

The select bibliography of Camões in English was compiled by Dr.
Luis de Sousa Rebelo whose assistance the editor gratefully
acknowledges.

The editor wishes to thank Maria Salema Vasconcellos for patient
typing and re-typing of a complex collection of material.

Translator's Preface

CAMÕES' INTERNATIONAL REPUTAtion rests on his epic; but even if he had not written *The Lusiad* he would merit a place among the great poets of the Renaissance. The present selection, framed by a few extracts from the epic and a long poem in the same form, is the only substantial English translation known to me from his lyrics apart from Sir Richard Burton's monument to unreadability ('Hard by a sunparcht, dure, esterile Mount') printed in London in 1884. *The Lusiad* was Camões' only work published during his life; adequate editions of his lyrics have appeared only in modern times. Of these I acknowledge particularly the annotated selection of Rodrigues Lapa (1978) and the larger editions of Álvaro Júlio da Costa Pimpão (1973) and Maria de Lurdes Saraiva (1980).

Camões used most poem types of the Italian Renaissance – here, the octave (*oitava*), the sonnet, the canzone (*canção*), the sestina (*sextina*) – and raised to equal status the Iberian folk lyric (*redondilha* in Portuguese) often based on a motto (*mote*) or theme of popular or other origin. The poet's unconventional emphasis on personal experience has encouraged a departure from the usual arrangement of the poems according to type, in favour of a supposed chronology: broadly, the poet's early life in Portugal; his voyages, with the death by shipwreck of the woman he loved; his last unhappy years in Lisbon.

Camões seldom gave his poems titles. When he did, they have been translated and distinguished by an asterisk. For ease of identification, the other poems have been given titles too. Notes on the poems and an index of first lines, both in English and in the original Portuguese, conclude this volume.

Translator's Acknowledgements

The present book owes its beginnings to celebrations in London in 1980 of the quatercentenary of the poet's death: for the occasion the Menard Press published a booklet of essays, poems and translations, to which I contributed an extract from *The Lusiad*. I was then invited to make a new translation of the epic: I responded by suggesting that I should translate instead a selection of lyrics, which are much less well known in the English-speaking world, and this was readily agreed. I submitted the first handful of translations to a competition organised by the British Comparative Literature Association: they won first prize and were published in *Comparative Criticism*, volume 6 (Cambridge 1984). My thanks are due first to those who thus set the book in motion; then to Mr L. C. Taylor, (at that time at the Calouste Gulbenkian Foundation), who commissioned it, to Mr Eugénio Lisboa of the Portuguese Embassy who advised on the selection, and to Professor Helder Macedo of King's College London who patiently answered many queries. All shortcomings that remain are my own.

Contributors

KEITH BOSLEY: has published several collections of poems, most recently *A Chiltern Hundred* (1987), and a good deal of translation, including *Mallarmé: The Poems* (1977), *From the Theorems of Master Jean de La Ceppède* (1983) and *The Kalevala* (1989).

SIR MAURICE BOWRA: (1898-1971) was Warden of Wadham College, Oxford and held office as Vice-Chancellor and Professor of Poetry. The range of his interests is indicated by his many publications which included *Periclean Athens*, *Pindar's Odes*, *Primitive Song*, *From Virgil to Milton*, *The Romantic Imagination*, *Poetry and Politics 1900-1960*, *The Heritage of Symbolism*, and the editing of the Oxford Books of both Greek and Russian verse. His *salons* were celebrated, and through them he influenced artistically-gifted undergraduates over several decades.

LIMA DE FREITAS: painter, engraver and writer, has participated in scores of exhibitions in Portugal and abroad, and has had one-man shows in his own country, in Paris (where he lived for eight years), in Warsaw, Copenhagen, Madrid, London etc. He was Director of the National Theatre in Lisbon for five years, has held professional appointments in Portugal and Denmark and is a Chevalier de L'Ordre du Mérite in France. He has written on a wide spectrum of art subjects, including geometry in art, labyrinths and symbolism. He is the foremost book illustrator in Portugal and has also illustrated books for publishers in Denmark, Poland and for the Limited Editions Club and Heritage Club in the United States.

HELDER MACEDO: poet and critic, is Camões Professor of Portuguese and Head of the Department of Portuguese and Brazilian Studies at King's College, University of London. He has been Secretary of State for Culture in the Portuguese Government (1979-80) and Visiting Professor of Portuguese and Comparative Literature at Harvard. His publications include four volumes of poetry, and books on Mediaeval Galician-Portuguese Lyric, Bernardim Ribeiro, Camões, Cesário Verde and studies of Almeida Garrett, Eça de Queiros and Jorge de Sena.

LUÍS DE SOUSA REBELO: is Emeritus Reader in Portuguese and the Calouste Gulbenkian Senior Fellow at King's College, University of London. He has been Associate Director of Studies at the École Pratique de Hautes Études, Paris. His books include *A Tradição Clássica na Literatura Portuguesa* (1982) for which he was awarded the Portuguese PEN Club Prize for Literary Criticism, and *A Concepção do Poder em Fernão Lopes* (1983).

KIM TAYLOR: founded the Ark Press in 1954, through which he has produced many fine editions, illustrated by international artists. He was an Editor of Graphis Magazine in Zurich, and Advisor and Designer for publications at The University of Texas (notably those of the Humanities' Centre) and lecturer in book design, typography and oriental art. He is author of *Wandering in Eden: Three ways to the East within us* and *Womankind: a Celebration*. Books he has designed have been included in both the Best Books of the Year in the United Kingdom and in 50 Best Books of the Year in the United States.

LUIS DE CAMÕES: *Epic and Lyric*

CONTENTS

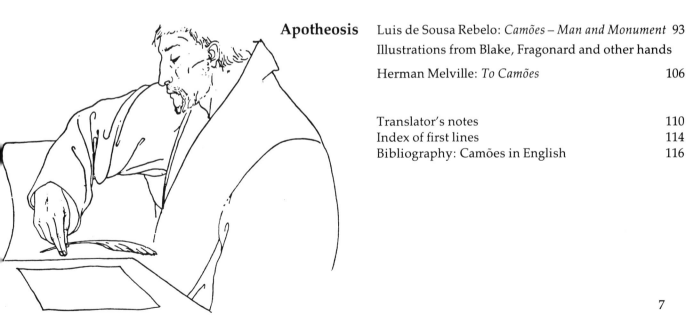

Epic

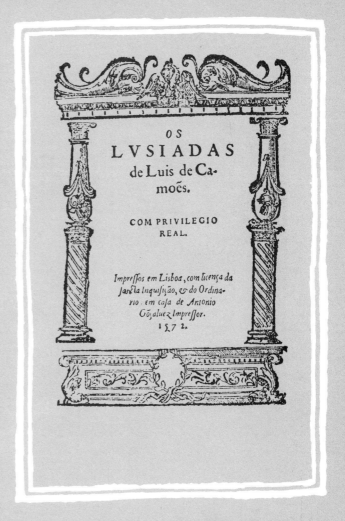

OS
LVSIADAS
de Luis de Ca-
moẽs.

COM PRIVILEGIO
REAL.

*Impreſſos em Lisboa, com licença da
Janẽla Inquiſição, & do Ordina-
rio . em caſa de Antonio
Gõſaluez Impreſſor.*
1 5 7 2.

Title-page of the first edition of Camões' epic *Os Lusiadas*, published
in Lisbon, 1572.

MAURICE BOWRA : *Camões and the Epic of Portugal**

T HE FIRST EPIC POEM WHICH IN ITS grandeur and its universality speaks for the modern world was written by a Portuguese. And this is right. For the achievement of Portugal in the years between the first expeditions of Prince Henry the Navigator in the fifteenth century and its incorporation in the dominions of Philip II in 1580 is one of the wonders of history, and marks with dramatic significance the transition from the Middle Ages to modern times and from a limited Mediterranean outlook to a vision which embraced half the globe. A small country, poor in population and in natural resources, ruled the seas and commanded an empire round the Cape of Good Hope to the East Indies and the China Sea. What Genoa and Venice had done in the Mediterranean, what Holland and England were later to do in the Indian Ocean, the Portuguese did in all the seas of the Eastern Hemisphere for a crowded century, although the voyage from Lisbon to Calicut lasted a year and was accompanied by all the perils of uncharted waters, shipwreck, scurvy, hostile natives and absence of communications. Of this far-flung dominion remains still survive in forts and churches built on African and Indian coasts, Abyssinian highlands and fever-stricken beaches of southern China, in

bronze figures of Portuguese musketeers from Benin and Burma, in words which have passed into Cingalese and pidgin-English, in stories of ancient fights which still echo in Malayan songs, in huge areas still under the Portuguese flag, in the memories of imperial splendour which still hover uneasily in the minds of the Portuguese and stir them at intervals to assert their old pride or to blame themselves for being inferior to their great ancestors. An achievement of this kind, equal in scale and enterprise to the Spanish conquest of the New World and even more costly in life and more dramatic in the brevity of its heyday, deserved the prize of epic song. By a happy chance it found a poet who was not only pre-eminently gifted to sing of it, but was himself singularly a man of his times, a soldier in foreign lands, a scholar of wide and humane learning, a man of charming sensibility and noble heart, a true son of the Renaissance as it developed by the Tagus and of that Portugal which looks out onto the Atlantic and has found in it 'the cradle and the grave of its glories'.

Luis de Camões (*c*.1524-1580) was disciplined by a life which had more than a just share of the disappointments and defeats upon which genius is supposed to thrive. In his youth, when he studied at the University of Coimbra then in the height of its glory, he laid up that classical learning which moulded his art and filled his mind with the seductive visions of Pagan antiquity. As a young man he fought in Morocco and paid with the loss of an eye for a knowledge of the Moorish character and methods of war. Imprisoned in Lisbon for tak-

* This essay is an abbreviated version of the chapter "Camões and the Epic of Portugal" in C. M. Bowra's book *From Virgil to Milton* (1945). The English translation used throughout is that of Sir Richard Fanshawe, published in 1655. C. M. Bowra wrote at a time when Portugal still ruled many overseas territories, now independent.

11

ing part in a street fight, he was released on condition that he served the King in India and he, who was already turning from pastoral poetry to the poetry of heroic achievement, was flung into a reckless, dangerous, humiliating life of adventure. In 1553 he sailed from Lisbon and was away for seventeen years. On his travels he learned the lure of the sea, which plays so magically through his poetry. In Goa he found so bitter a disillusionment that he called it 'the step-mother of all honest men', but there he studied the lives of men, Christian and Hindu, marked the habits of the Indians, and mastered what he could of their geography, history and religion. He took part in military expeditions up the Malabar Coast and to the Red Sea. In 1556 he sailed east by way of Malacca and the Molucca Islands to Macao, where a grotto still keeps his memory and his name. Two years later he began his long, painful, interrupted voyage home. He was shipwrecked off the mouth of the Mekong River in Siam, and lost all his possessions except the manuscript of his poem to which he clung while he swam to land. In Goa he was again imprisoned, nor, when he was at last released, were his troubles at an end. He was delayed at Mozambique by illness and poverty, and he did not reach his beloved Lisbon till 1570. For years he had been at work on his great epic, *Os Lusiadas*, and in 1572 it was published. Legends have clustered round Camões' last years, and though it is now doubted whether he died in beggary, he had few comforts or consolations. In 1578 he heard of the appalling disaster of Alcazar Kebir, where King Sebastião and the flower of the Portuguese nobility (blessed by the Pope and fortified with a sacred banner, an arrow of St Sebastian, and the sword of old Affonso Henriquez, the first king of Portugal) were slaughtered by the Moors in Moroccan sands. In 1580 Camões died. The date has a tragic significance; for it was the year in which Portugal lost its independence to Spain. Before Philip II came in state to Lisbon to assume his inheritance, Camões had written to the Captain-General of Lamego: 'All will see that so dear to me was my country that I was content to die not only in it but with it'. His actual death may have been caused by the plague, but his work was done, and he had no wish to live any longer.

Scholar and soldier, humanist and man of the world, Camões was uniquely fitted to write the epic of Portugal. His knowledge was gained both from books and from life. His aim was to write for his own country a poem which should rival the *Aeneid* in artistic perfection and in national aim. He understood what he was doing; for he was an accomplished Latinist, who knew the Latin poets with a lover's intimate knowledge, and hardly a page of *Os Lusiadas* fails to awake some echo of them. He seems not to have known Greek, but he probably read Homer in Lorenzo Valla's Latin version, and to a man of his imaginative sensibility the vision of Hellenic splendour was bright enough in its Roman reflections. He was equally well acquainted with Spanish and with Italian and had learned the new style of writing which had come from Italy to Portugal. His decision to write an epic was in accord with his times; for even in Portugal, which had lacked epics in the Middle Ages, the cultivated Antonio Ferreira was urging poets to celebrate their country's history in epic song. Camões' poem was the product of its age equally in its classical reminiscences and in its national subject. His companion for some twenty years, it was intended to rival the epics of antiquity in art and to surpass them in truth and nobility. Camões begins with a conscious challenge to Virgil, with his own version of *arma virumque cano*:

> As armas e os Barões assinilados.
> (Canto I, verse 1, line 1)

> Arms and the men above the vulgar file.
> (Fanshawe)

His theme, he claims, will put Odysseus out of court; his Vasco da Gama will equal Aeneas in renown. He addresses the King of Portugal as Virgil addresses Augustus, and he is confident that his poem will become famous through the world.

Camões attempt to rival Virgil in epic poetry provides an instructive comment on the literary theories of the time, and especially on Vida's *Ars Poetica* published at Cremona in 1527. Vida lays down rules for a poet's education, and chance willed that Camões should follow them. In his excellent classical education, in his youthful acquaintance with country life in the valleys of the Mondego and the Tagus, in his experience of love and his experience of war, in his distant travels and in the knowledge of the world which he gained from them, he learned in abundant measure the lessons which Vida demanded. Since it is likely that he knew Vida's work and accepted its main postulates, we need not be surprised that he followed up his natural advantages with a close study of Virgil's text and was proud to make his poem Virgilian in more senses than one. Only by such means, he seems to have felt, could he rise to the height of his great theme. Such a belief was of course dangerous. The poet might follow his model too closely and do imperfectly what had already been done perfectly. But Camões did not fail. He gives new meanings to ancient themes, adapts old devices in a fresh and brilliant way, and applies the ideal of Rome with creative originality to his own day. He sets a distance between himself and Virgil

both in his metre, which is the *ottava rima* of Ariosto, and in his language, which, despite its classical air, is singularly lucid, direct, natural and swift. When we first read him, we hardly think of Virgil; so well has Camões absorbed the principles of epic construction and used them in his own way. Later we see how great his debt is, but such is his mastery of his material that his personal impress is on almost everything. Indeed at times he uses his model so freely that he seems to criticise it and to think that he can better it. The result is that we compare *Os Lusiadas* with the *Aeneid* not as an imitation with an original, but as one poem with another of the same kind.

The title *Os Lusiadas*, or *The Sons of Lusus*, challenges comparison with *Iliad* and *Aeneid*. It is a conscious classicism. The sons of Lusus are the Portuguese who were believed to be descended from Lusus, the eponymous hero of Lusitania. The word, which Camões learned from Portuguese poets who wrote in Latin earlier in the sixteenth century, conveys an air of distinction, of association with the ancient world, and shows Camões' wish to set his poem in the Roman tradition. It also shows something else. The poem is not, like the *Aeneid*, called after a man but after a people. Though the *Aeneid* is the poem of Rome, it is so indirectly; *Os Lusiadas* is much more directly the poem of Portugal and of what Camões calls 'the illustrious Lusitanian soul'. Just as Virgil conveys the wider prospects of Roman history in prophecy, vision and works of art, so Camões, on a much more generous scale, builds the history of Portugal round his central theme. He lays equal emphasis on his chief hero, Vasco da Gama, and on the people of which Gama is so typical a representative. His voyage is a turning-point in the long heroic story. In it the Portuguese find an outlet for the qualities which they have already shown to be theirs, and their success in it proves that once their power has entered these new fields, nothing should be able to withstand it.

If we compare the construction of *Os Lusiadas* with that of the *Aeneid*, we can see what special advantages Camões gained. First, since the actual story of Portugal receives far more attention than Virgil gave to that of Rome, the poem is more obviously a national epic and has a greater variety since it covers different centuries and spreads to different continents. The great men whom Camões celebrates are typical of their country in their characters and their fortunes. Foremost are the great kings whom he names in his Introduction and whose achievements he tells later. These figures of noble royalty, who challenge comparison with Charlemagne, take first place in the creation, defence and expansion of Portugal. The first is the crusader Affonso Henriquez who founded the Portuguese kingdom by freeing the country round Lisbon from the Moors. In him Camões indicates the divine protection which watched over the birth of Portugal. For in the battle of Ourique, where Affonso defeats the Moors, he is sustained by a vision of the Cross before the battle, and after it shows his gratitude by composing the royal arms from the five shields of the kings who have been killed and the thirty pieces of silver for which Judas betrayed Christ and which are now in part redeemed. The life of this king is of long struggles against enemies within and without his territories. He is the typical crusader, the champion of Christendom and the scourge of the heathen, and his career shows under what favourable auspices the young country fought its way into existence. Of his successors the two most remarkable are Affonso IV and João I. Affonso IV is the protector of Portugal against Moorish invasion and the gallant ally of Spain against the vast African army which invades Europe and is defeated at Salado. His courage has its hard and even its brutal side, and his reign is marred by the cruelty with which he permits the hideous murder of his son's mistress, Inez de Castro. He is the typical mediaeval king, compounded of different elements, formidable and worthy of his title 'o bravo'. João I, the founder of the House of Aviz, starts a new age. After becoming king of a disintegrated country and having to restore order at home, he defeats Spain and carries his victorious armies to Africa, where he begins the expansion of Portugal overseas by the capture of Ceuta. The last king whom Camões presents is João II, who conceives the project of reaching India by the Cape of Good Hope and prepares for Gama's quest. Through these great figures Camões marks the progress of Portugal from a small state on the Tagus to a great empire stretching across half the world.

A second advantage which Camões found in his subject and in his historical method was that he was not concerned with an imaginary past but with recorded history or with a present of which he was himself in part a witness. Instead of having to describe battles in a lost heroic age and to resort to imaginary archaeology, he can fill his story with convincing and realistic details which are based on fact. Himself a soldier, he saw the past through his own experience. Homer has a like air of actuality, but Homer's scene is narrower than that of Camões. Camões draws on the admirable Portuguese historians, Ruy de Pina, Barros and Castanheda, as Shakespeare drew on Holinshed, and though he keeps to the facts, he sees them with his own imaginative and discerning eyes. There is no sham romance and no anachronism about his mediaeval battles:

> Heads from the shoulders leap about the field;
> Arms, legs, without or sense or master, fly.
> Others, their panting entrails trailing, wheel'd,
> Earth in their bloodless cheek, death in their eye.
>
> (111, 52, 1-4)

When he came to his own times he used his personal observation with splendid effect. He had seen strange weapons and methods of war in the East and must have helped to operate the prized military inventions of the age. In short and vivid phrases he calls up the attempt of the Samudri of Calicut to destroy Pacheco's fleet with Greek fire, the bulwarks and palisades of Malacca, the catapults and mines used in the defence of Diu, the arrows which the wind turned back upon the Persian archers at Ormuz, the poisoned darts of the Javanese, the elephants of Hydal-Khan, the flag of Portugal raised high over captured Columbo. This is war as it was fought in the sixteenth century.

This actuality pervades the poem. Since the Portuguese empire lay on and across the seas, it is right that its poet should know them well and be able to write finely about them. From the first words about Gama's fleet at sea,

> They now went sailing in the ocean vast,
> Parting the snarling waves with crooked bills;
> The whisp'ring Zephyr breath'd a gentle blast,
> Which stealingly the spreading canvas fills.
>
> (1,19,1-4)

it is clear that the poet is a sailor. This knowledge of the sea appears at every stage of Gama's voyage, in strange phenomena like the Southern Cross, the Fire of St Elmo, and the water-spout, in all the horrors and dangers of voyages in unknown waters:

> Sudden and fearful storms the air that sweep;
> Lightnings that with the air the fire do blend;
> Black hurricanes, thick nights, thunders that keep
> The world alarm'd, and threaten the last end.
>
> (V,16,3-6)

It is a sailor who admires the use of the astrolabe, who describes how the ships' bottoms are scoured of the limpets and weeds which have collected on them or how the scurvy makes the sailors' flesh swell and putrefy in the mouth, who tells how a storm falls suddenly on the fleet and breaks the main-mast of a ship, while the half-dazed crew lower the top-sails or climb into the rigging. When Virgil describes a storm and the emotions which it awakes in Aeneas, he discovers many incidental beauties, but his words are those of a landsman who has a deathly horror of shipwreck. Camões writes as a man of action who knows the dangers all too well but also knows how they are to be encountered.

The newly discovered lands were as full of marvels as the new seas. The geographical decoration which Vida recommended from maps and globes, if not from travel, was for Camões largely a record of what he himself had seen and noted with eager, curious eyes. The visual variety of his poem is much enhanced by his skilful choice of vivid details. Sometimes they come from common life, like the sails made of palm-leaves at Mozambique, or the striped cotton clothing of the men who work them. At other times they take on a romantic majesty, as when the people of Melinde wear purple caftans and silken clothes, and their king, on whom Camões spends three stanzas, has a golden collar, velvet sandals covered with gold and pearls, and a richly wrought dagger, while a servant holds an umbrella over him as he rides in his royal barge to the music of twisted trumpets. In contrast to him are the simple ways of ordinary natives, the Kaffirs delighted by the crystal beads, scarlet caps and little bells with which the Portuguese try to do barter, the women riding lazily on oxen, the presents which they bring of sheep and poultry, their

15

songs and dances which awake echoes of Virgilian shepherds in the poet. In India above all there was much to capture Camões' fancy. He gives a vivid picture of the Samudri's palace with its spreading pavilions and pleasant groves, of the Samudri himself who sits in state while an old man, kneeling on the ground, gives him a betel-nut to chew, of the monstrous Hindu deities with their violent colours and many limbs. When he turns to the farthest East he is hardly less circumstantial and notes much of interest that he has heard or seen, the cannibal Gueons who tattoo their flesh, the Indo-Chinese who believe that after death their souls pass into animals, the strange people of Pegu said to be born from a woman's union with a dog. He conjures up the scenes of this remote geography, the nutmeg-pigeons of the Banda Archipelago, the sandal-trees of Timor, the submarine plants of the Maldive Islands, the volcanoes of Tidor and Ternate, and the Great Wall of China. Without seeming to stray from his main theme Camões touches on almost the whole East as his age had discovered it.

Into this vast setting with all its variety and colour Camões introduces real men. His hero, Vasco da Gama, is to be a rival to Virgil's Aeneas:

> Th' illustrious Gama in the rear I name,
> Who robs the wandering Trojan of his fame.
>
> (I,12,7-8)

The claim is well founded. If Aeneas' voyage led to the foundation of Rome, Gama's voyage not only began the Portuguese Empire in the East but altered the history of the world by revealing to a self-contained Europe vast prospects of enterprise in Africa and Asia. Gama's discovery was almost as important as that of Columbus, and his actual voyage was a finer feat of scientific navigation. If Aeneas founded the universal empire of Rome, a similar claim might be made for Gama and Portugal, as Venus says when she reveals the earth to him:

> Thus has thou all the regions of the East,
> Which by thee giv'n unto the world is now.
>
> (X,138,1-2)

The performance and its results were on a truly Roman scale. Camões chose his subject well, but his choice of a hero created difficulties. Virgil could fashion his Aeneas as he pleased and make him a symbol of the Roman character, but Gama could hardly fulfil the same function in the same way for Portugal. His record was known to everyone. He was no knight-errant; he was not even so great a soldier as Pacheco or Albuquerque. A man of extraordinary ability, of great determination and foresight, he lacked the more glamorous qualities of heroism. Even the success of his voyage somehow detracts from its romance. Its conclusion, exciting enough at the time, has not in retrospect the wild improbability of what befell Cortés and the Pizarros. Even the India which he discovered was not so strange or so unknown as the realms of Montezuma and the Incas. To make a hero of so real a man as Gama called for considerable dexterity.

The most striking quality of Camões' presentation of Gama is its truth to history. If we leave out the mythological elements, which serve a separate purpose, the voyage follows the route to India which Gama discovered and which Camões knew from his own experience. In the story he selects salient events, as he is bound to do, but he does not add or invent, and even his selection bears some relation to the account given by one of Gama's own crew in his log-book. The main episodes are few — the fight at Mozambique, the lucky escape from Mombasa, the welcome at Melinde, the storm in the Indian Ocean, the arrival at Calicut, the inconclusive negotiations with the Indian ruler and the departure. Almost any of these might have been disguised and dramatised into something more heroic or romantic, but Camões is content to tell of each very much as it happened. He does not even exaggerate Gama's rôle. The result is different from anything done before in epic. At first sight readers used to Ariosto or even to Homer and Virgil may find *Os Lusiadas* a little flat. The adventures of the Portuguese are so lifelike that we may miss something in them, until we see that this was Camões' intention and that he aims at securing an effect of truth and reality. He believed that his truth was as interesting as fiction and his poem was written on that principle. In his quiet way he has created a noble and serious poetry. His Gama is not a great warrior like Achilles or even like Aeneas. His qualities are more subtle and more practical. His genius is for success, and despite reverses and accidents, despite his own mistakes and miscalculations, he succeeds and reaches India. The qualities demanded of him and displayed so conspicuously by him are not those of the great Portuguese kings and viceroys. Gama is great because he carries out successfully a difficult task as he has been ordered. He is a new kind of hero, with something of the astuteness of Odysseus and the perseverance of Aeneas, but these are not his chief claims. What counts most is that he is a great servant of Portugal and displays its characteristics in a highly effective way. Camões knew that there were other noble types, and in their own place he praised them. Gama is one type among others. He is not like Aeneas the representative of a nation's soul, but a real man who is interesting and admirable for his own sake and for the sake of the country which bred him.

Camões choice of subject and of hero brought him many advantages and gave a modern and realistic character to his poem. His subject was undeniably up to date, and if he succeeded in making a great poem of it, he might well claim to be a Portuguese Virgil. But the theories and taste of his time demanded more than this. It was not enough to rival Virgil in a new kind of heroic narrative; he must keep many of Virgil's characteristics and decorative effects and especially he must satisfy a scholarly taste for learned allusions. Just as Virgil adapts themes and phrases from Homer, so Camões decked his poem with echoes and hints of classical myth. No doubt he did so with eager enthusiasm; for the world of classical fancy and history was among his first and most enduring loves. Modern taste, however, may find it hard to appreciate his less concealed classicisms, his deliberate imitations of Roman poetry, and his mythological references. His head and heart were so full of ancient verse that at times he seems too eager to reproduce it and looks almost a translator. But this is to misunderstand him. His classical references and reminiscences are more than what his public expected of him, more even than his own indulgence in a devoted loyalty; they are his tribute to Latin civilisation, his confession of faith in what he believed to be most important in the European inheritance, his acknowledgement of a debt to the past and to the language which his own Portuguese so resembled that he made Venus claim that there was hardly any difference between them:

> And in the charming music of their tongue
> Which she thinks Latin with small dross among.
>
> (I,33,7-8)

The revival of learning in the fifteenth and sixteenth centuries was much more than an academic or even a literary matter. It gave the world something that it lacked, a strong sense of secular life. To all matters not theological the precedents of Greece and Rome gave a new zest and confidence. The ancient achievements in government, in science and in the arts inspired the men of the Renaissance with a new outlook and new impulses. They felt more at home in the world now that they knew something of their own historical origins. So Camões stresses the connection of modern times with ancient, the unbroken continuity of the tradition, and the many similarities between Portugal and ancient Rome. In the great plan of his poem the classical tradition has a special place; for the new contact of West and East brought to the fore the special qualities which Europe owed to antiquity. The Roman heritage, quite as much as any differences of religion, differentiates Europe from Asia and Africa. The East, despite its wealth and its immemorial past, is in the last resort uncivilized because it lacks this humanising force. Camões was deeply conscious of this, and it explains the emphasis which he gives to the ancient world.

In transforming his Virgilian model to suit his times and his country Camões, naturally enough, made free use of similes. Of all the devices of Greek poetry the simile has had the most remarkable career. Unlike many oral poets, Homer uses similes on a large scale and puts into them those experiences and scenes which he could not put into his heroic narrative. Virgil followed him closely and seldom went beyond his range of subjects. Camões takes up the tradition and shows how well he understands the real function of the simile. Its chief use is to provide a break in the narrative by suggesting something outside its events which illustrates them. The point of comparison varies, but usually it is a mood or tone and makes us think that there is something more in what happens than appears in the mere account of it. Some of Camões'

similes come from books, others from life, but they are always fresh and apposite and give the relief and illumination which a simile should. When he had to describe an unfamiliar phenomenon, he found that a novel simile helped him to be more exact. He had, for instance, seen a waterspout and been much impressed by it; so he makes Gama describe one, carefully and accurately, to the King of Melinde. A thin vapour rises in the air and begins to revolve, then throws out a tube to the sky, grows larger and draws up water from the sea while a dark cloud hangs over its top. The strange phenomenon demands precise description, but to relate it more closely to common experience Camões adds a simile:

> As a black horse-leech – mark it in some pool! –
> Got to the lip of an unwary beast,
> Which, drinking, suck'd it from the water cool,
> Upon another's blood itself to feast;
> It swells and swells, and feeds beyond all rule,
> And stuffs the paunch, a rude unsober guest:
> So swell'd the pillar, with a hideous crop,
> Itself, and the black cloud which it did prop.
>
> (V,21,1-8)

The leech, swelling with blood, is an excellent parallel to the swelling waterspout. There is even a point in the beast which has sucked it up unexpectedly; for the waterspout itself is highly unexpected. To convey the significance of this strange new sight Camões draws his simile from common rustic life. His method is Homer's; for Homer often compares great events to small without detracting from their grandeur. But the subject and its details are Camões' own. From this piece of simple observation he makes a parallel which is not only visually but emotionally relevant; the waterspout is sinister and frightening, and so too in its own small world is the leech. The simile is in the true epic tradition, fresh, apposite and effective.

By such means Camões adapts the Virgilian technique and gives a Virgilian character to his poem. But this would not be enough for the theorists of epic in his age. He must also follow his model in relating his human events to some scheme of things and provide a metaphysical or theological background. In other words he must have divine personages in his poem, as Virgil and Homer had before him. Lucan indeed omitted the gods from his *Pharsalia*, but he was censured for it by Petronius and his example was not followed. The epic was expected to give a comprehensive picture of life and would fail in this if the gods were left out. It might also fail to reach the right heroic tone; for to this the gods of Virgil indubitably contribute. When Camões wrote an epic on the Virgilian model, he must decide what to do about the gods. They must be present in some form, but it was not easy to decide in what. Since Camões lived in a Christian age, he might perhaps be expected to use some kind of mythological machinery based on Christianity. No doubt this would have been acceptable in the sixteenth century when few would have felt, as Boileau did in the seventeenth, that any such attempt led to a falsification of divine truths and that to set the figures of Christian belief in such a poem was

Du Dieu de vérité faire un dieu de mensonges.

Even so there was a serious artistic objection to such a procedure. The God and the Saints of Christianity are not easily placed in a heroic poem; for, as Dryden says, 'the machines of our Christian religion, in heroic poetry, are much more feeble to support that weight than those of heathenism'. The alternative was to keep the Pagan gods and to give them a new significance. It is true that they had long ago ceased to be worshipped and that some might regard them as devils or creations of the Devil. But the revival of learning had given them a new life. For the moment many accepted them at least as creatures of noble fancy. So Camões, true to his love of antiquity, chose to introduce them, to make them appeal aesthetically to the imagination and at the same time to give them a serious place in his main scheme.

It is sometimes assumed that Camões treated the Olympian gods as literary conventions, as figures who represent abstract qualities or natural forces. Such was the method of the seventeenth century when Boileau identified Minerva with prudence, Venus with beauty, Jupiter with thunder and Neptune with the sea. The method is more than familiar, but it is not that of Camões. It is true that his Neptune is a god of the sea and his Mars of war, but even these allegorical figures take on some kind of personality when the first holds court in his submarine palace or the second strikes his spear-shaft on the floor of Olympus in angry defence of the Portuguese. Camões' Venus is much more than beauty, his Jupiter than thunder, his Bacchus than wine. His mythology is far less abstract and arid than that of the seventeenth century; it reveals a deeper and more sympathetic understanding of the antique gods than Corneille felt when he demanded their presence in poetry:

Qu'on fait d'injure à l'art de lui voler la fable!
C'est interdire aux vers ce qu'ils ont d'agréable.

Between Camões and this kind of decoration there lies a great dispute about the whole relation of heathen beliefs to a Christian society, a dispute which left a place for the gods of heathendom only by making them sacrifice much of their reality. Camões still breathes the air of the Renaissance and believes that the ancient gods are worthy of honour. He does not indeed follow Pico della

Mirandola who worked out a system to equate the doctrines of Plato with those of the Church. For Camões' concern is not intellectual but aesthetic; his gods and goddesses come not from philosophy but from poetry. He is more like Raphael, who in his *Parnassus* displayed the divine figures of antiquity as a counterpart to those of Christianity. They were for him as supreme in the arts and sciences as the Church was in religion and morals; they were even real, in the sense that they embodied forces powerful in the human heart and in the conduct of life. In the Renaissance the two worlds could exist side by side. Camões accepted the paradox and made the most of it.

As in the *Aeneid* the main conflict in heaven is between Venus and Juno, so in *Os Lusiadas* it is between Venus and Bacchus. Jupiter holds the final decision but stands aside from the struggle. It is fated that the Portuguese shall come to India, but Bacchus is determined to postpone the evil day for as long as possible and to put every hindrance in their way, while Venus is no less determined to give help. The issue, which pervades the poem, is made clear in the first scene on Olympus, which shows Venus and Bacchus at loggerheads. The first crisis comes on the African coast when Bacchus sets out to create mistrust and hatred in the Moors for the Portuguese and to lure his enemies to destruction. At Mozambique he disseminates dark rumours, but is foiled by Gama's watchfulness. So he makes the fleet come to Mombasa, where he disguises himself as a Christian and raises a Christian altar which naturally deceives the men whom Gama sends to report on the situation. Camões indulges a quaint fancy when he makes Bacchus worship at this altar:

> from whence it doth ensue
> That the false god came to adore the true.
>
> (II, 12, 7-8)

The Portuguese believe that the inhabitants are Christian and try to enter the harbour, but, to their great surprise, their ships will not move – because Venus and her Nymphs prevent them. The whole scene is of a radiant beauty. The goddess and her Nymphs are as lifelike as if they came from Virgil or Ovid. But the episode has its symbolical significance. It shows the conflict between dark powers of suspicion, hatred and deceit which fight against Gama, and other powers, which save him from destruction and may justly be regarded as providential. Superhuman forces are engaged on both sides; the spirits of West and East, of civilisation and barbarism, are at work. Nor is all this mere fancy; it has a basis in history. The Portuguese really believed that there were many Christians in Africa who would welcome them. Even the intervention of Venus is not too removed from fact; for as Gama was entering the harbour at Mombasa, a false manoeuvre by one of his ships made the Moors think that their plot was discovered, and their agitation put the Portuguese on their guard and made them leave for Melinde.

The second crisis between Venus and Bacchus takes place in the Indian Ocean. Determined to prevent the fleet from reaching India, Bacchus invokes the powers of the sea to send a storm. The fleet is in great peril, but Venus intervenes in time and calms the waters. The storm is real, even historical, if we assume that Camões has transposed to this time and place the fearful storm which fell on Gama in the Atlantic when he was on his way home, and into it Camões has put details gained from his own experience. The storm is the last obstacle which the explorers have to pass before reaching their goal. Having suffered from the malignity of men, they now suffer from the malignity of the elements. Once again Venus and

Bacchus stand for supernatural powers that help or obstruct the Portuguese. The spirits of East and West include powers of nature as well as of man. Bacchus creates violence and disorder in the elements; Venus restores calm and order. The divinities stand for something not easily labelled but revealed in their actions. Venus, with Mars to help her, is a protecting power of Western order, Bacchus is the opposite. The beneficent forces of the world, which arise from civilisation, are no less displayed in nature; the evil forces, which fill men's hearts with hatred and distrust, are akin to the violent natural powers which discoverers have to face. In Venus and Bacchus Camões gives a fundamental conflict in the world, a strife between opposites in which one or the other must yield. In the result Venus wins. Bacchus wastes himself in intrigues and fails; Venus rewards those whom she supports and gives them peculiar delights in her Island. In his Pagan mythology Camões has found new symbols to display the real issues that he sees in Gama's voyage. The discovery of India is important not only for its historical results but because it is a great victory for harmony and order in physical nature and in the human heart.

Such scenes show what the antique gods were for Camões. In them he found figures of delight and beauty, brilliant contrasts to the world which he saw about him. They are powers of the spirit which give light and glory to human achievements and grant an unreckonable reward to those who honour them; they are the forces which have created the best elements in European life as Camões knows it. Their memory must have comforted him through many dark hours among the hateful intrigues of Goa or on the stricken shores of Africa. In their own way and in their own place they are real. Camões believes in them and honours them. Free from the theological inhibitions of the Middle Ages and hardly touched by the Counter-Reformation, he works out his own way of bringing the Olympian gods into his poem. What even Ariosto does not do, Camões does gaily and confidently. His divinities play an indispensable part in his poem, and it would be vastly poorer without them. Through their interactions with men it moves, like most great epics, at two levels. The human action has its own grandeur, but it acquires greater dignity because the gods have a part in it. The grim struggles of the Portuguese discoverers are one side of the picture; the other side contains all that the gods represent, the glory and the delight that they bring, the order which they create. In adhering to this convention of epic poetry Camões wins a triumphant success. Like Correggio and Raphael, he understands the ancient gods and sees their meaning for his own time.

Gama's voyage to India, and the history of Portugal in which it is a turning-point, provides Camões with his main theme. They give him the heroes which he needs for his national epic. But he seems to have felt that to confine himself to such themes was to make his poem too grave and too austere, that it needed some diversion of a different kind. Much of *Os Lusiadas* comes from a world which owes little to Virgil and bears no resemblance to the starker kinds of heroic poetry. Yet even in this Camões might have claimed that Virgil provided him with a precedent. For Virgil had introduced into his heroic frame something of the romantic poetry of Alexandria and made use of fancies which were outside the heroic scope. So Camões felt himself justified in giving part of his epic to a kind of poetry which might seem to be far removed from it. The most popular poem of his time was the *Orlando Furioso* of Ariosto, published in 1516. This great work belonged to a great tradition. It followed naturally where Boiardo had led the way. For lovers of poetry in the sixteenth century the Italian chivalrous epic, brilliant, gay, romantic, debonair, pictorial, was what mattered most. It was admired and loved by Camões, who felt that his own poem must find some relation to it and show its superiority. If his readers expected from him something like the *Orlando Furioso*, they must learn that he offered something truer and nobler. In his Introduction he stresses this three times, when he claims that his subject is truer than the stories of Rodomonte, Ruggiero and Orlando, that his Portuguese kings match Charlemagne, and that the Twelve of England are as good as the Twelve Peers. He challenges a great and popular poetry, and he suggests that, although what he tells is true, it is in every way as interesting and delightful as the imaginations of Ariosto.

In attempting to combine this kind of poetry with his heroic story Camões set himself a difficult task. Despite its historical connections with heroic epic, chivalrous epic moves in another sphere of the spirit and makes few calls to serious ambition or high resolve. Camões adds much colour and life to his poem by using some themes of chivalrous epic, but he introduces them circumspectly with a proper regard to their relevance in their new place. Some themes indeed he omits. The miraculous, which Boiardo carried to such superb lengths, is missing from any action of Camões' human characters. Even love is confined almost to the single story of Inez de Castro, which is based on history and told in a tragic spirit with a high classical style. But there were other themes which could be adapted to a new setting without spoiling the balance of the poem. For instance, the chivalrous epic was much attached to jousts and tournaments with their proper accompaniment of injured damsels championed by gallant knights. Such a subject appealed to Camões' tender, dreaming, amorous soul, and he makes his own use of it.

Another less tractable theme of chivalrous epic is the brutal giant who frightens men by his revolting appearance and inflicts hideous tortures on them – like Ariosto's Galigorante, who from his hidden haunt in the sands traps unwary wayfarers of both sexes and eats them. He is almost the ogre of fairy-tale, and his kind might seem to have no place in the discovery of India. Yet on it Camões has built one of his most renowned and most original episodes, the appearance of Adamastor. When the fleet reaches the southernmost point of Africa, on a calm night a cloud rises and grows until it is seen to be the figure of a giant. Camões spares no details of his repellent aspect, from his scowling face, squalid beard, and hollow eyes to his filthy hair, black mouth and yellow teeth. He is as large as the Colossus of Rhodes, and his deep, ugly voice makes the hair stand up on those who hear it. Like any other giant, he abuses the Portuguese for breaking into regions which he regards as his private domain and forbidden to all strangers, and proceeds to foretell horrors and destruction to them. Then he tells his own story, which is of course one of injured innocence. He sought marriage with Thetis, but was foiled by a trick. When he believed that she was his, he found that his embraces were wasted on a rock. There is a gross, ogreish bestiality about his ardour when he thinks that he has won the object of his desires:

> With open arms, far off, like mad I run
> To clip therein my joy, my life, my sweet:
> And, clipt, begin those orient eyes to kiss,
> That face, that hair, that neck, that all that is.
>
> (V,55,5-8)

Like other monsters, Adamastor is extremely sorry for himself and hates everyone. When he disappears with loud weeping and a howl over the sea, he shows that, despite his ugly threats, he is defeated. His character and appearance come largely from chivalrous epic and through it from fairy tale, but Camões has transmuted him into something more remarkable and more significant.

Adamastor is convincing because he is related to fact and because his forecasts of evil belong to history. He foretells disasters, all of which occurred in the regions round South Africa in the years after Gama's voyage. The first, ironically appropriate in its victim and specially pleasing to Adamastor, is the storm that brought death to the first European to round the Cape, Bartolemeu Dias. The second is the death of the great Viceroy, Francisco de Almeida, who paid for the destruction of Quiloa and Mombasa by falling on African soil in a chance fight with natives when he was on his way home to Lisbon. The third is the fearful catastrophe which befell Sepúlveda, who had been governor of Diu and was returning with his beautiful and loved wife, Leonor. They were shipwrecked and, after hideous treatment by the natives, saw their children die before they themselves died of starvation and thirst. Adamastor dwells on the horrors which await them:

> Starv'd shall they see to death their children dear,
> Begot and rear'd in so great love. The black
> Rude Caffirs, out of avarice, shall tear
> The clothes from the angelic lady's back.
> Her dainty limbs of alabaster clear
> To heat, to cold, to storm, to eyes worse wrack
> Shall be laid naked, after she hath trod
> Long time with her soft feet the burning clod.
>
> (V,47,1-8)

The Cape of Storms, which Adamastor personifies, was indeed to bring many agonies and disasters to the Portuguese in their early voyages round it. It is not without reason that he prophesies woe to Gama and his successors:

> This know: as many ships as shall persevere
> Boldly to make the voyage you make now,
> Shall find this point their enemy for ever
> With winds and tempests that no bound shall know.
>
> (V,43,1-4)

When Camões wrote, these perils were familiar, and Adamastor might well seem to represent a hideous and hostile force of nature. The ogre has become something more formidable than a figure of fairy tale.

Just as Bacchus symbolises the difficulties which the Portuguese meet on their journey to the East, so Adamastor symbolises a natural obstacle, the passage round the Cape of Storms, the point where East meets West and disasters are common. As the ancients believed that no man could safely sail beyond the Pillars of Hercules, so in the sixteenth century some may have believed that even after Dias had rounded it, the Cape set a natural limit to sailing. The Portuguese pass this limit and have to pay for it. Their triumph over it is part of the whole process by which they bring order and civilisation to remote places. Camões shows this in his own way. When he makes Adamastor one of the Giants, the companion of Enceladus, Aegeus and Centimanus, and the enemy of Jupiter, he indicates that he belongs to an old chaotic state of things which Divine Providence has now decided to control. The myth is carried further in Adamastor's amorous pursuit of Thetis. She is a sea-goddess, and she refuses his advances. The sea is to belong not to primaeval powers like him but to the Portuguese. Adamastor's real inheritance is the rock which he finds in her place, thick with scrub and thorn, a fit emblem of his Antarctic world. Even he himself is turned to earth and has become the

Cape; it is only his phantom that appears to Gama. The sea, which he once sought as his bride, flows round him and increases his anguish. Camões' myth presents the triumph of the Portuguese over untamed forces of nature and their reward in becoming masters of the sea. The horror which the vision of Adamastor arouses is based on a natural fear of going too far and has a real relation to experience. The grisly and revolting phantom is an apt symbol of the horrors which may well appal those who break into waters where no men have sailed before.

In his management of his poem Camões shows a remarkable independence. If he means to rival Virgil, he knows that it must be in his own way. In particular, he assumes that a poet can state his own opinions, which Virgil hardly ever does explicitly or directly. The sixteenth century accorded a position of honour to a poet and listened with respect to what he had to say; it even expected him to have views on matters of serious and general interest. These might be given implicitly, as Virgil gives his. But the poets of chivalrous epic had evolved a simpler method of speaking in their own persons. By such means Boiardo and Ariosto were able to produce many interesting effects in fanciful arguments on such topics as the faithfulness of wives or the proper uses of dishonesty. They were also able to touch on graver matters, as when Ariosto rises to noble eloquence in his apostrophe to the Furies who devastate Italy, or his contrast of the barbarity of contemporary war with the courtesies of old times. Ariosto usually sets such passages at the beginning of a canto as a prelude to what follows. Camões followed this tradition, but altered its details to suit his different aim. He does not confine such passages to the beginning of a canto, nor himself to general reflections. Sometimes he philosophises on general matters, sometimes he speaks about himself. In particular, he begins and ends his poem with long addresses to King Sebastião. In his Introduction of eighteen stanzas he commends his poem to the King. It is a statement of literary aims as well as an appeal to the King to be proud of his people's achievements. Its length and elaboration show that Camões treats his subject with a seriousness unfamiliar in Ariosto. He underlines the main subjects and the national qualities of his poem; he shows what kind of an epic he claims his to be. The Introduction creates expectations of what is coming and gives the poet's conception of his poem.

In Canto X, Camões closes his poem with lessons to be learned from it. His advice to the King is tactful and respectful but courageous and clear. He urges him to reduce the rigour of the laws, to promote experienced men to his Council, to see that the religious orders keep fasting and discipline and avoid worldly ambitions, and to look after his army. The advice, given in this liberal spirit, was needed. The young King lacked experience and judgment, and he had recently come under Jesuit advisers who inflamed his natural fanaticism. Camões felt so strongly that a poet was the voice of his nation that he was prepared to risk any displeasure that his frankness might win for him. He felt that something was wrong with the Portugal of his day:

> Nor know I by what fate, or duller chance,
> Men have not now that life and general gust
> Which made them with a cheerful countenance
> Themselves into perpetual action thrust.
>
> (X,146,1-4)

He could not but contrast the heroic Portugal of his poem with the actual Portugal that he found on his return from India. Something seemed to be lost, and history justifies him in thinking so. The expense of energy and life in the conquest of India had been too great for a small country, and the high spirit of Gama's generation had vanished. Camões calls on the King to restore it. In his poem he has presented the vast scope of Portuguese heroism and the great parts played by her Kings; it is for King Sebastião to be worthy of his ancestors and to revive the ancient spirit.

For Camões the King of Portugal is more than a national monarch. He rules an empire from the rising to the setting sun, and he, much more than the Emperor or the Most Christian King of France, is the champion of European Christendom:

> You fair and tender blossom of that tree
> Belov'd by Him, who died on one for man,
> More than whatever Western Majesty
> Is styled Most Christian or Caesarean.
>
> (I,7,1-4)

He is a terror to the heathen who are half ready to submit to him:

> On you with fixed eyes looks the cold Moor,
> In whom he reads his ruin prophesied;
> The barb'rous Gentile, viewing you, is sure
> You'll yoke his neck, and bows it to be tied.
>
> (I,16,1-4)

A poem which begins in this spirit and then describes the heroic doings of Portugal in the past must inevitably end on a heroic note. Such was indeed expected by the King. Sebastião believed that he was called to conduct a crusade against the heathen and, after abandoning a project for such a war in the East, turned his mind to Africa and made his first military reconnaissance on the Moroccan coast. The idea of a crusade was more than welcome to his spiritual advisers, and the King himself dreamed of reviving chivalrous ideals. The Turks were advancing into the heart of a Europe rent by religious wars. No wonder that Sebastião, blessed by the Pope, felt that he had to play his part. So too did Camões. His poem ends with an appeal to the King to take the field in Africa:

> Making Mount Atlas tremble at your sight
> More than at that of dire Medusa's head,
> Or putting in Amplusian fields to flight
> The Moors in Fez and black Morocco bred.
>
> (X,156,1-4)

All influences converged to the same tragic end, and the old imperial Portugal perished in the butchery of Alcazar Kebir. It is the irony of Camões' life that the ideal which he proclaimed and which seemed to be justified by history had outlived its strength. His country had become weaker than even he knew.

Camões conception of kingship is related to the central idea of his poem. In the Portuguese he sees champions of civilisation and Christianity against the corrupt forces of Islam and barbarism. What this meant to him can be seen in the emphasis which he gives to it in Canto VII when Gama's fleet has just reached Calicut. Once again he develops a theme from Ariosto, who had hoped to find champions of Christendom in Francis I, Maximilian, Charles V and Henry VIII. The unity which he imagined proved a mirage, and when Camões wrote, European Christianity was even more divided. In words of savage irony he rebukes the Germans, among whom Luther's work was beginning to show results, for inventing a new creed and fighting against the Pope instead of against the Turks; the English, whose King claims to be King of Jerusalem but who forgets the celestial Jerusalem and turns his sword against the servants of Christ; the French, whose King calls himself 'Most Christian' but who allies himself with the heathen, as Francis I did with Suleiman the Magnificent against Charles V; the Italians, who waste their lives-in wealth, pleasure and indolence, and whose vices make them easy victims of tyranny. Camões' denunciation of Europe is a criticism of Ariosto's hopes. He shows how little trust could be placed in these rulers and their countries. When he wrote, the position was worse than in Ariosto's time. The Council of Trent in 1563 and the Massacre of St Bartholomew in 1572, the year in which *Os Lusiadas* was published, were signs of the European discord. So though not all Camões' complaints are quite contemporary, they are none the less relevant. In this discredited European company Portugal alone keeps up the fight:

> But whilst, mad people, you refuse to see,
> Whilst thirst of your own blood diverts you all,
> Christian endeavours shall not wanting be
> In this same little house of Portugal.
>
> (VII,14,1-4)

The conviction that his country is the real champion of Christendom is a driving force in Camões' poem.

Camões desires nothing less than a European crusade against Islam. Its first object must be to drive the 'dogs' out of the Holy Sepulchre. But he is moved by other aims than this. He feels compassion for the peoples of the Balkans and Asia Minor who are under Turkish rule:

> The Thracian, Georgian, Greek, Armenian
> Cry out upon you, that ye let them pay
> – Sad tribute! – to the brutish Alcoran
> Their Christian children, to be bred that way.
>
> (VII,13,1-4)

His real sense of European culture and his love for Greece as its cradle filled him with indignation that these other, hardly less holy, lands should be in the enemy's corrupting grip. He even holds out a worldly bait to the divided peoples of Europe that their efforts will be rewarded by splendid plunder, for the East is full of gold. To this project Camões

sees one great obstacle: while Islam is united, Europe is divided. Let it close its ranks, and it will conquer; for not only is its cause just, but modern inventions are on its side:

> That Hellish project of the Iron Age,
> Those thunderbolts of war, the cannon-ball,
> At Turkish galleys let them spit their rage,
> And batter proud Constantinople's wall.
>
> (VII,12,1-4)

Though it is hard to imagine a return to the spirit of Cœur de Lion or S Louis in the sixteenth century, and though the discoveries of the explorers had turned men's eyes to worlds remoter than the Levant, Camões was not alone in preaching such a crusade. The Popes approved of it, and the battle of Lepanto in 1571, when Don John of Austria destroyed the Turkish fleet, showed that victory was by no means impossible. If a united crusade had been undertaken in a serious spirit, Eastern Europe might have been saved from three centuries of servitude. The Portuguese might well feel that they at least bore their full share of a European duty when they fought against Islam in Africa. It was their ruin, but there is a tragic magnificence in the intensity of their effort to take on the enemy alone. Camões had reason to be proud of his people, and he was moved by more than merely national pride.

This conception of a European mission and of the need for a modern heroism is no mere dream. Camões knew what he was saying and was fully aware not only of what such ventures cost but of the real objections that can be made to them. He had himself seen that such successes are won only at a great price and may often seem not to be worth it. He had himself suffered from the corrupt agents of Portuguese imperialism, and his natural love of ease and pleasure often made him protest against the sufferings and humiliations which life in the East exacted. At times he pauses to lament his own misfortunes, and at the end of Canto I he suggests that they are almost too heavy for him to bear:

> Where may a frail man hide him? in what arms
> May a short life enjoy a little rest,
> Where sea and land, where guile, the sword and dearth
> Will not all arm 'gainst the least worm of earth?
>
> (I,106,5-8)

His passionate attack at the end of Canto VIII on the corrupting effects of the desire for money is surely based on his own experience in the Indies. Camões was not a man to hide his sorrows, and at times he forces them on our notice in a sudden outburst of melancholy or complaint. He was certainly without illusions about what the ideal of empire meant in practice.

Camões even shows how strong a case can be made against an endeavour like that of the Portuguese in India. Just as Adamastor prophesies horrors and disasters, so, when the fleet is about to sail from the Tagus, an Old Man of venerable mien cries out upon the whole undertaking and denounces the vanity of fame and the horrors and cruelties which the desire for empire breeds. In ten great stanzas he thunders against the imperial ambition, its cost and its demoralising influence. Almost every one of his arguments has some force in it – that glory is a mirage, that the pretence of spreading religion brings only more horrors, that the prospect of making money is largely illusory, that the Ishmaelite will always prove superior in cunning, that it is madness to seek foes afar when there are other foes near enough at home, that moral corruption follows the lust for glory:

> Fell tyrant of the soul! life's swallowing wave!
> Mother of plunder and black rapes unchaste!
> The secret miner and the open grave
> Of patrimonies, kingdoms, empires vast.
>
> (IV,96,1-4)

This is no mere rhetorical display. Into it Camões has poured much of his own experience, of the bitterness and disillusion which his lyrical poetry expresses so poignantly. It is the other side of the imperial venture, and its inclusion in the poem adds greatly to its depth and truth. Just as Virgil sets his heroic actions against a background of doubt and uncertainty, so Camões sets his against the misgivings and disillusions which must have assailed both him and many of his contemporaries. These things are true, and he does not deny them. Indeed he throws much of his own feeling into them and gives them the appeal of painful, personal knowledge. But he feels that they are not the whole truth nor the most important part of it. The Portuguese mission justifies its ruinous cost by the qualities which it calls into action and the good that it promises to the world.

Os Lusiadas is in many ways the epic of Humanism. The new vision and the new values which came with the revival of learning found in Camões a poet singularly fitted to sing of them. He is a Humanist even in his contradictions, in his association of a Pagan mythology with a Christian outlook, in his conflicting feelings about war and empire, in his love of home and his desire for adventure, in his appreciation of pleasure and the demands of his heroic outlook. But he is above all a Humanist in his devotion to the classical ideal and in his conviction that this was the living force in the imaginative life of Europe in his time. He equates Portugal both with Christianity and with the classical tradition. The Counter-Reformation and the Inquisition hardly touched him, and such small concessions as he made to them do not affect the character of his work. His poem covers a wide range of experience because it was written by a man who was open to many kinds of impression and had a generous appreciation of human nature. Though he has much of the magnificence of the Renaissance, he tempers it with a taste which always knows when to stop. His conception of manhood is fuller and more various than Virgil's. He has indeed something of Homer's pleasure in the variegated human scene and, like Homer, he knows that there can be more than one kind of noble manhood. *Os Lusiadas* is a true product of that Europe, Christian and classical, of which Camões was so faithful and so distinguished a son.

Selected passages from *The Lusiad*

The Battle of Aljubarrota

*The epic opens with Vasco da Gama sailing up the east
coast of Africa. Entertained by the king of Malindi (in
modern Kenya), he gives him a history of Portugal. Here
he describes the Battle of Aljubarrota in which the
Portuguese, though heavily outnumbered, defeated the
Castilians in a battle for their country's independence.*

To arms! shrilled the Castilian bugle-blare
Horribly, wildly, hugely, frightfully:
The sound was heard as far as Finisterre;
Guadiana switched its waves as if to flee;
The Douro heard, and that land beyond where
The troubled Tagus runs towards the sea
And mothers terrified by its alarms
Gathered their little children in their arms.

How many faces shed their colour there
As to the heart's aid comes the kind blood's flow!
For in great perils oftentimes the fear
Is slighter than the peril, or seems so
Though it is not: this is because the sheer
Rage to attack, to conquer the harsh foe
Numbs us before the great and grievous loss
If limb or life itself were torn from us.

The uncertain combat starts now to be joined
And first wing moves on first wing opposite:
Some rise to the defence of their own land
And others to their hopes of gaining it.
The first whose deeds will one day be renowned
Is great Pereira, on whom all virtues sit:
He strikes down, he confronts, then sows the mould
With those who want what is not theirs to hold.

Already through the thick air come the screaming
Javelins and arrows, all kinds of shot fly;
Under the hard and thunderous hoofs of steaming
Horses the ground shakes, hollow valleys cry;

Lances thud home and rend, till all is teeming
With clattering falls that stun and stupefy
And the foe rallies, swells, engulfs the slim
Force of fierce Nuno, and is put to shame.

Against him, see! his brothers band together
(How foul, how cruel!) but he is not afraid:
Little it is to seek to kill a brother
For one who King and country has betrayed
And of these traitors there is many another
In the first squadron which is now arrayed
(How freakish!) against brothers, kin and home
As in the civil wars of ancient Rome.

O noble Coriolanus, you, Sertorius,
Catiline, and you other shades of old
Who against your own countries with inglorious
Hearts took up arms, unnaturally bold:
If where death only is victorious
In Pluto's deepest pits you now are rolled
Tell him that even among the Portuguese
Sometimes there are betrayers such as these.

The first of our men here are giving ground:
So many of the foe upon them fall!
Nuno is there, who in the hills that bound
Ceuta's port is the strongest lion of all
Who seeing horsemen ringing him around
Running across the fields from Tetuan's wall
Hounding him with their lances, is annoyed
At the disturbance but is undismayed.

Seeing it he sees them, but his fierce race
And wrath conspire to make him scarcely one
Who would turn tail: instead, into the mass
Of spears he hurls himself, though more come on.
Likewise the gallant knight, who stains the grass
With foreign blood; but there some of his own
Must perish also, all their courage lost
To gallant hearts before so great a host.

31

Good King John felt the insult, the close shave
Nuno was bearing and, wise captain, ran
All the way there, saw for himself and gave
By his presence, his words, heart to his men.
Just as a mother lioness, fierce and brave
Who leaves her cubs unguarded in the den
Feels that, while she is out in search of food
The Barbary shepherd has borne off her brood:

Raging she runs, she roars, and with her voice
Stuns all the hills and sets them quivering.
So good King John with others of his choice
Comes running, bringing aid to the first wing:
'O mighty comrades, in whom I rejoice
Great knights whose like no prince has power to bring
Defend your lands, for all our hopes, our chances
Of liberty are hovering on your lances.

'You see me here your King, yet one you know
Who through the lances, arrows, panoplies
Of the foe runs, and is the first to go:
Fight on, fight on, you true-born Portuguese!'
The generous Chief Warrior spoke so
And taking up his lance, four times he weighs
Then thrusts it hard, and from this single thrust
Many were tilted over, breathed their last.

For see, his men being kindled all anew
By noble ignominy and worthy flame
To find among their gallant hearts one who
Will conquer perils in the martial game
Press on. Hot iron is stained a bloody hue:
Mails they smash first, then the breasts under them
And thus they take and give wounds equally
As though it cost no suffering to die.

Many they send to lap Styx' bitter taste
Into whose bodies death and iron have ploughed:
The master of Santiago sinks in haste
Who fought long bloody and till now unbowed;

That other master too, who laid great waste —
The lord of Calatrava, cruelly proud;
To the Pereira traitors too is given
Death, so that they betray both fate and heaven.

And many common folk without a name
As well as nobles go to the abyss
Where the three-throated dog with jaws aflame
Lusts after souls to that world passed from this
And the more fully to subdue and tame
The enemy's fanatic haughtiness
They seized the topmost banner of Castile
And ground it with the Lusitanian heel.

Here the fierce battle rages more intense
With death, with carnage, blood, hullabaloo:
The multitude of those who fade from hence
Have changed the very flowers from their own hue.
Now they turn tail, now die, and now relents
The fury, and the lance-thrusts have grown few
And the Castilian king is now defeated
As he can see, and of his purpose cheated.

He leaves the field now to the conqueror
Relieved that he has not been left to die:
The remnant follow him, propelled by fear
No more with feet to march, but wings to fly
And in their deepest heart they shed a tear
For death, for all their squandered property,
For woe, dishonour, for the bitter bile
Of seeing others triumph with their spoil.

And some of them are cursing and blaspheming
The one who first into the world brought war
And others make the target of their blaming
The one whose rabid bosom thirsts for more
Who to take what is not his, by his scheming
Exposes to the depths the humble poor
Leaving so many mothers, so many wives
Without sons, husbands, hopeless for their lives.

Victorious John stayed the accustomed days
Upon the field, parading gloriously
And then with offerings and pilgrimages
Gave thanks to him who gave him victory.
But Nuno who desired no other ways
Among the folk to leave his memory
Than by his arms none ever could withstand
Slips through the lands of Tagus and beyond.

His destiny comes to his succour well
By making his achievement match his thought:
The land that fronts the Vandal citadel
Yields him both spoil and conquest, cheaply bought.
The Andalusian banner of Seville
And various lords is in a moment brought
Under his heel, flung down without defence
And grateful for the Portuguese advance.

By these and other victories for long
The people of Castile were sore bested
But peace that now was wished for by the throng
The victors gave to those who bowed their head
For the great Father who in all is strong
Decreed that these two warring kings should wed
Two most illustrious, gracious English girls —
Princesses, fair of face with golden curls.

(*Lusiad, canto 4, stanzas 28-47*)

Against Empire

Vasco da Gama tells of a venerable old man who harangued his fleet as it left Lisbon on the voyage to India. The old man is speaking.

'At home the foe threatens to overwhelm
But you pursue one in a distant land:
Is it for him you drain this ancient realm
And far beyond its strength make it expand?
Doubt and a taste for danger keep your helm
That you may rise in fame and then may stand
Flattered as lord who rules with sovereign sway
India, Persia, Araby, Africa?

'Accursed be the first who in the world
Set sail upon the waves in a sound ship!
Into the deepest hell he should be hurled
If there is justice in the law I keep.
May no high sentence ever be uncurled
Nor sounding strings nor quick invention leap
That your renown or memory should flourish:
Rather with you your name and glory perish!'

(Lusiad, canto 4, stanzas 101-2)

From Equator to Cape

Vasco da Gama recalls the experience of sailing down the Atlantic, an encounter with a whirlwind, a skirmish with hostile Africans and the apparition of the giant Adamastor, spirit of the Cape of Storms.

By now we had discovered out in front
In the new hemisphere a bright new star
Unseen by other folk who, ignorant
At certain times had been unsure of her:
We saw the part that is less brilliant
And for its fewer stars is not so fair
From the fixed pole where nobody has found
Whether new land begins or the seas end.

So through those regions making our career
Which Phoebus touches twice on his patrol
Bringing two winters and two springs each year
While running from the one to the other pole
Through calm, through tempest, through dull heavy air
Where angry Aeolus makes the sea still roll
We saw, despite the best of Saturn's daughters
The two Bears dipping into Neptune's waters.

To dwell upon the many shapes of doom
The sea holds, which man's reason cannot bear –
The sudden thunderstorm, the frightful boom
The lightning flash that sets the air on fire
The black squall and the long night full of gloom
The thunderclap, world-splitting in its roar –
Would be hard work as well as wrong to tell
Even though my voice rang like an iron bell.

I have seen cases where rough sailors, who
Are schooled only by long experience
Always regard a thing as right and true
According to their senses' evidence
While those who take a more considered view
Apply their knowledge or sheer common sense
To secrets of this world more deeply hid
And judge them false, or else misunderstood.

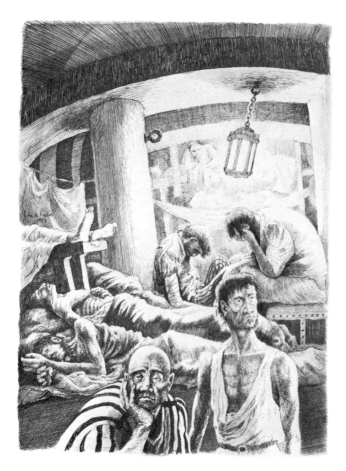

With my own eyes I saw (and do I look
Like one deceived?) a vapour-wisp begin
To rise up in the air, a subtle smoke
Begotten by the gale, to turn and spin
From when a tube toward heaven's topmost peak
Was seen to soar, so tenuous, so thin
The eye could not perceive it readily:
Fashioned from cloudy stuff it seemed to be.

And it continued growing, growing still
Till it was stouter than a tall ship's mast:
Here it grew narrower, there broader while
Into its throat great gulps of water passed.
As it bobbed up and down upon the swell
A cloud grew at its top end thick and fast
Bulging and billowing greater and greater
The more it fattened on its freight of water.

As when a purple leech is seen to cling
To the lips of a beast that turns aside
Imprudently to drink at a cool spring
Slaking its wild thirst on another's blood
Gulping, with each gulp growing, fattening
Filling out there and swelling round its load:
So the tall column, filling out, exceeds
Itself, so too the black cloud which it feeds.

But when its appetite begins to wane
The foot upon the deep is seen to lift
And hover in the heavens, dropping rain
To water all the shallow waters left:
The waves it took it gives to waves again
But of salt savour they are now bereft.
Now let the scholars search their libraries
To learn of nature's secrets such as these!

If the philosophers of old, from land
To land searching out secrets that were theirs
Had found the wonders I myself have found
Spreading my sails to winds from all quarters

I have seen clear as day St Elmo's Fire
Regarded by sea-going folk as holy
In stormy weather full of dark and dire
Tempest, of lamentation, the wind squally.
No less a marvel, certain to inspire
Terror in all – it terrified us truly –
Was to behold the clouds with a long pipe
Sucking the Ocean's mighty waters up.

What great accounts they would have left behind!
What influence of signs, knowledge of stars!
What prodigies and what great properties!
And all would be the sober truth, no lies.

But now the planet that in the first sphere
Dwells, on her circuit five times hastening, now
With half her crescent face and then entire
While our fleet cleft the waves, had made a show;
When from the crow's nest calls a mariner
On first beholding it: 'Land ho! Land ho!'
All hands leap to the deck in noisy haste
Eyes scanning the horizon to the east.

Rather as clouds before us are arrayed
Shapes that become substantial and are hills;
We dress the anchors ready, long since weighed
And once we have arrived we furl the sails;
And so that we may stand in better stead
Of where we are in such remote landfalls
With the astrolabe, newest of instruments
A wise invention full of subtle sense

We disembark where there is room therefore
From where the men go scattered all about
Eager to see what strange things lie in store
Upon this land where no one has set foot;
While with the pilots on the sandy shore
To find out for ourselves what is this spot
I stay behind to take the sun's position
And comprehend the general situation.

We find that we have now completely passed
Capricorn with its horns and fins, the sign
That stood between us and the icy blast
Of the Antipodes least known to men.
Then of a sudden, by my men held fast
I see a stranger coming, black his skin
Whom they by force had taken as he tried
To gather honey on the mountainside.

His eyes flash white, his face begins to twitch
As one whose case was never so extreme:
We do not understand each other's speech
For he is more uncouth than Polypheme.
I go to show him what made Jason rich
Fetching the fleece whose metal reigns supreme;
Fine silver too, and spice whose breath is fire –
But none of these inflamed the brute's desire.

I have him shown some baubles, worthless odds
And ends – some crystal beads he can see through
A few small bells, mere peas in brazen pods
A cap of scarlet, quite a cheerful hue.
I saw then by his gestures, by his nods
At sight of these his joy and wonder grow:
I let him take them all and go, and he
Makes for his village not so far away.

But on the morrow, bodies all agleam
Naked and black as night, his villagers
Pour down the rugged hillsides in a stream
In search of baubles such as those he bears:
So tame and so companionable they seem
To our Fernão Veloso that he dares
To go and see the customs of the land
With them, beset by bush on either hand.

Veloso's right arm is his confidence
His arrogance cannot foresee a fall;
But now that a long time has gone by since
I had a sign from him that all was well
Anxiously waiting on an eminence
For the adventurer, there on the hill
He emerges: towards the sea his steps are bent
Coming in greater hurry than he went.

Coelho's skiff set off in a trice, advances
To take him, but before it can come near
An Ethiop impertinently pounces
Upon him, so that he cannot get clear.
Another and another leap: his chances
Veloso doubts, with none to help him there;
I rally then, and while we ply the oars
A band of black men suddenly appears.

Arrows and rocks and stones in a dense cloud
Shower upon us an unrelenting rain;
Nor did they, launched upon the wind, fall wide
For this leg wounded there still gives me pain;

But we as persons who were sorely tried
Gave our attackers so much more again
That in additioin to our caps they got
More scarlet souvenirs as like as not.

Veloso now being safe after the raid
Then we withdraw and row back to the fleet
Seeing the ugly malice, the harsh mood
Of folk so bestial, rough, degenerate;
From whom no better knowledge could be had
Of India on which our hearts were set
Than that it still lay very far beyond:
So once more I shall spread sail to the wind.

At that Veloso heard a man declare
As all his shipmates broke into a smile:
'Hey, friend Veloso, coming down – I dare
Say – was worth more than going up that hill!'
'Surely,' replies the bold adventurer;
'But when so many dogs were on the prowl
And closing in, I kept my wits about me
And hurried on, for you were here without me.'

He went on to relate to us that when
That peak was passed, the blacks of whom I speak
Would not allow him to press further on
Threatening to kill if he did not turn back;
And when he did, they laid an ambush then
So that our rescue would prompt their attack
And once they had dispatched us, all our treasure
Would be their spoils to sample at their leisure.

Now – to continue – five suns had passed by
Since we had gone from that place, cleaving through
Waves of a hitherto uncharted sea
While favourable winds upon us blow;
When one night as we take our ease, carefree
But keeping watch upon the cleaving prow
A mightly cloud that darkens all the airs
Above our unsuspecting heads appears.

So terrible it came, so frightfully
Swelling, it filled our hearts with a great dread
While the dark sea far out with muffled cry
Seemed to be slamming some reef with its head.
'O Power,' I uttered, 'you who dwell on high!
What divine threat, what mystery has led
This climate and this sea to show its form
Which looks to me far more than a mere storm?'

I had not finished when a figure rose
Before us in the air, robust and hale
But of misshapen and enormous size
With bulbous face and beard abominable;
Its eyes were sunken and its posture was
Dreadful and foul, its colour earthen, pale;
Matted with soil its bristling hair; beneath
Its mouth gaped black, displaying yellow teeth.

So great its limbs were, that I am concerned
For you to know as truth what you are told
That this was Rhodes' Colossus new returned –
One of the seven wonders of the world;
Its voice was huge and horrifying, churned
Up from the depths as though the ocean growled:
All our flesh creeps, all our hair stands on end
To see that vision and to hear that sound.

It said: 'Bold people, you who undertake
More than so many in the world great matters;
Who to vain ventures tirelessly awake
Wage wars so cruel, deal so many slaughters:
Since the forbidden boundaries you shake
And dare to navigate my distant waters
Which I for so long now have kept and held
Unploughed by strangers, by myself unsailed;

'Since you come here to search the mysteries
Of nature and the fluid element
Whose revelation no great man calls his
However noble, immortal his intent;

Hear now from me the allotted penalties
Awaiting you who are too impudent
Upon the high seas and upon the land
Which you will conquer with relentless hand.

'Know that whatever vessel may intrude
As you do now, and on these seas be brave
Will find no friend within this latitude
Where wild winds blow their worst and tempests rave;
And on the first fleet that shall sail, that would
Carve out a passage through this restless wave
I shall deal such an unexpected blow
That what they feared will bow to what they know.

'Here will I take, if I am not misled,
Total revenge on who discovered me;
Nor will your stubborn trust by this one deed
Receive the fullness of the penalty:
No, each year will your ships be visited
(If reason serves my senses properly)
With rack and ruin, so that out of all
Disasters death as least bad will befall.

'The first and glorious viceroy, whose high fame
And fortune even heaven will celebrate
Will find in me a new, eternal tomb
Decreed by God from his high judgement seat;
Here with his proud, rich trophies he will come
From his encounter with the Turkish fleet
And with my punishments will come no less a
Threat from the sack of Kilwa and Mombasa.

'Another will come too, his fame uncommon,
Generous, gallant-hearted and in love
And with him he will bring the handsome woman
Whom Love in a great shower of blessing gave:
This pair a sad plight and dark fate will summon
Into this realm of mine; they will survive
A cruel shipwreck so that fate's illwill
May heap upon them troubles greater still.

'They will see hunger claim their little ones
Out of such wealth of love conceived and born;
They will see rough and grasping Africans
Strip the fair lady, all her clothing torn;
Her splendid limbs as clear as precious stones
By calm, by cold, by wind they will see outworn
From planting till there seemed to be no end
Delicate feet upon the burning sand;

'And more those eyes will see, allowed to break
Free from so many ills, so much anguish –
The pair of wretched lovers driven back
Into the burning and remorseless bush:
There, after softening the very rock
With tears of grief, with utter woe awash
Their souls will with a last embrace have risen
Out of their lovely and most wretched prison.'

But the horrific monster's prophecies
Boomed on to tell us all that lay in store
Till I stood up, said: 'Who are you? The size
Of that vast frame amazes me for sure.'
With a great grin and rolling back its eyes
And letting out a terrifying roar
It answered in the heavy, bitter voice
Of one who was not speaking out of choice:

'I am that great cape wrapped in mystery:
The Cape of Storms in your tongue I am called;
I was unknown to Strabo, Ptolemy,
Pomponius, Pliny and all those of old;
Here the whole coast of Africa is by me
Rounded off with a headland none beheld
That out towards the Antarctic pole extends
That your foolhardiness so much offends.

'I was among the first our mother bore –
One of the giants, not known for our devotion;
My name is Adamastor; I made war
On him who sets young Vulcan's rays in motion:
Not that I might pile mountains, but offshore
To dominate the billows of the ocean
I sailed as a sea-captain out to where
Neptune's fleet sailed, the god I sought to scare.

'Love for the lofty wife of Peleus
Drove me to such a daring enterprise;
My love for Thetis, watery princess,
Turned me from all goddesses of the skies.
One day I saw her in her nakedness
With Nereids on the beach: I felt her seize
My will with so much power that even today
No greater over my desire holds sway.

'Since there was no chance that I might attain her
With the unsightly grossness of my face
I resolved then by force of arms to gain her
And to her mother Doris make my case.
On my behalf she seeks to entertain her
But Thetis, smiling truth as much as grace
Replied: "Can a nymph's passion be enough
When measured up against a giant's love?

' "And yet, for the ocean to deliver us
From so much war, a way out I shall find
That this and my good name may bear no loss."
My messenger had gone; such words remained.
I was not one to fall for tricks like this
(How great the darkness that makes lovers blind!)
But still my throbbing breast was quite filled up
With longing for the Nereid, and with hope.

'Foolishly I withdrew now from the war
And on a night, as Doris gave her word
The lovely form appears to me from far
Of Thetis, white, her matchless body bared:
Like one possessed I ran from far to her
With arms flung wide to clasp one who inspired
Life in this body, and began to kiss
Her fair eyes, kiss her tresses, kiss her face.

'I know of nothing loathsome like the tale!
Thinking my loved one was in my embrace
I found within my arms a rocky hill
Bristling with scrub, a wild and craggy place.
Being up against a cliff face cheek by jowl
And hugging it for her angelic face
I was no more a man, but drained of life –
A dumb, still cliff beside another cliff.

'O nymph, the handsomest of Ocean, since
You reckon now my presence but a low thing
Was it too hard to keep up this pretence
And make me a hill, a cloud, a dream, a nothing?
Angry I leave, and wellnigh maddened hence
By grief and shame that used me for their plaything
In search now of another world I go
Where none will laugh at my lament and woe.

'My brothers by this time had been defeated
And placed in mysery where no help avails;
That the vain gods might see their triumph completed
Some have been buried under various hills:
Since against heaven main force cannot be pitted
I, as I went about weeping my ills
Began to feel the blows fate was preparing
Lining its forces up against my daring.

'My flesh has been transformed into hard earth
As craggy cliffs my bones are newly set;
These limbs you see before you, and this girth
Across these waters have been parcelled out;
And finally the gods, no doubt for mirth
Changed my enormous bulk to this remote
Cape, and to crown my torments, Doris' daughter
Still laps about my base with all this water.'

He told, and with a miserable roar
Suddenly disappeared before our eyes;
The black cloud dwindled, and the sea afar
Echoed obscurely with deep-sounding cries.

Raising my hands towards the holy choir
Of angels who had steered our destinies
I begged God to keep us from each disaster
That had been prophesied by Adamastor.

(Lusiad, canto 5, stanzas 14-60)

42

Europe Rebuked

As the voyage approaches its destination, the poet reflects on the faith of Europe.

And now they see that they are close to land
Which was the apple of so many eyes
With Indian streams lapping its every strand
And Ganges too, the earthly paradise.
Up now, strong people, whose unconquered band
Will lift the victor's palm into the skies:
Now you have come, now here before you stretches
The land that overflows with wealth and riches.

To you, O Lusitanians, I say
That to you such a small plot has been given
Not only in the world but equally
In his sweet fold who rules the curve of heaven —
You who not only are not turned away
By danger from subduing the unshriven
Nor yet by greed or disobedience
To Mother Church, whose mansions are far hence.

So few and yet so strong, you Portuguese
Who by your puny numbers are not cowed
Who have afforded many deaths to blaze
One Law of everlasting life abroad.
Thus heaven which decides our fate decrees
That you, although so few, have been endowed
To do great deeds as guardians of the holy:
How high, O Christ, do you lift up the lowly!

Look at the Germans, those conceited cattle
Whose pasture is of such a huge extent
Who with the one in Peter's Chair did battle
And now new shepherd and new flock invent:
Look at them, busy with the sabre's rattle
Who in blind error still are not content
To take up arms against the heathen Turk
But labour to shake off the rightful yoke.

43

Look at the hard-faced Englishman, self-styled
King of the ancient city, that beloved
Shrine by the shameless son of Ishmael ruled
(Who from the truth saw honour so removed?):
Taking his ease among the northern cold
He fashions a new faith that none has proved
Baring his sword before the men of Christ
Not to recover land he once possessed.

Meanwhile a false king holds against his might
Jerusalem, that city here below
While he spurns in the holy Law's despite
The high Jerusalem to which we go.
Now you, unworthy Frenchman, I indict:
You sought the name 'Most Christian' – wherefore? No:
Not to defend it, give it your protection
But to attack it, bring about destruction.

Do you think that Christian lands are yours to claim
Although you have so many of your own
Careless to hear your holy ancient name
Spat on by Arab and barbarian?
Their lands are where the sword must find its fame —
On those who mock the Church's cornerstone:
From Charlemagne and Louis you have land
And name, which you lack courage to defend!

What shall I say of those who tread the ways
The world brings, and in idleness go rotten
Who in cheap pleasure wallow all their days
And all their ancient virtue have forgotten?
For a strong people breeds hostilities
And out of these is tyranny begotten:
You I call, Italy, sunk in a gulf
Of countless vices, turned against yourself.

O miserable Christians! It would seem
That you are those same teeth which Cadmus sowed
Which though the offspring of a single womb
Tear at each other, strike each other dead:

Have you not noticed that the holy tomb
Is in the hands of Cain's united brood
Who come to you to take your ancient land
And reach for glory with a bloody hand?

You see them acting as their laws require
But gladly too, as to the manner born
Taking arms in a restless host to pour
On peoples who love Christ their fire and scorn:
Today the savage Furies never tire
Of sowing hateful tares among your corn.
Beware! From danger you are never free
When they and you are both your enemy.

(Lusiad, canto 7, stanzas 1-10)

44

In his *Portugal* (1957), Roy Campbell says he had Camões' works with him during the Second World War when posted, with a squad of the King's African Rifles, to the same strip of isolated, swampy coastline near Cape Guardafui where the shipwrecked Camões wrote Cante IX of *The Lusiad*. Camões' experience, Campbell declares, makes him 'the soldier's poet *par excellence*' and he saluted Camões in this sonnet, *To Camões*.

To Camões

Camões, alone of all the lyric race,
Born in the angry morning of disaster
Can look a common soldier in the face.
I find a comrade where I sought a master
For daily, while the stinking crocodiles
Glide from the mangroves on the swampy shore,
He shares my awning on the dhow, he smiles
And tells me that he lived it all before.
Through fire and shipwreck, pestilence and loss,
Led by the *ignis fatuus* of duty
To a dog's death – yet of his sorrows king –
He shouldered high his voluntary Cross,
Wrestled his hardships into forms of beauty,
And taught his gorgon destinies to sing.

ROY CAMPBELL

Lyric

RHYTHMAS
DE LVIS DE CAMOES.
Diuididas em cinco partes.

Dirigidas ao muito Illustre senhor D. Gonçalo Coutinho.

MIHI TAXVS

Impressas com licença do supremo Conselno da geral
Inquisição, & Ordinario.
EM LISBOA,
Por Manoel de Lyra, Anno de M.D. Lxxxxv.
A custa de Esteuão Lopez mercador de libros.

Title-page of Camões' poems, published in Lisbon, 1595.

HELDER MACEDO : *Camões and his Lyrics*

N O POET LESS DESERVED TO BE CAST as a national monument than Camões. Those of his works which speak in a new voice to successive generations reveal the same adventurous and questing spirit that placed Portugal in the vanguard of Europe's overseas expansion. The stereotyped image of monumental greatness denies actual qualities of a man who preferred the risk of seeking unknown truths to the comfort of received Truth.

His finest work is subtly subversive. He adopts Renaissance models (Ovid and Virgil, Dante and Petrarch, the Bible and Platonicism) and uses their idioms to very different ends. Camões owes his poetic mentors, especially Petrarch, the apprenticeship which enabled him to make the dark Portuguese language sing with a luminous Italian eloquence. Traditional rhetoric applies a familiar template to an individual genius which would have been unintelligible or perceived as dangerous at a time when puritanical morality and repressive religiosity were spreading.

The Portugal of Camões' youth was tense with contradictions. Roman Catholic Orthodoxy had to contend with Lutheranism and Calvinism, a tradition of humanist tolerance with the emergence of crypto-Judaism. And even after the institution in 1536 of the Inquisition in Portugal, after lengthy negotiations and diplomatic pressure from Spain, religious repression was tempered by an official sense that severity should be balanced by enlightened understanding. The Grand Inquisitor (the Cardinal-Prince Henry) had been a disciple of the Flemish humanist Cleynaerts (Nicholas Cleonardus) and, as the King's brother, his education suggests the point to which the Portuguese crown was imbued with a humanist spirit.

In the very year in which the Inquisition assumed full powers (1547) King John III established a new College of Arts in Coimbra, assembling the pleiad of Portuguese humanists who had contributed to the prestige of the universities of Paris and Bordeaux. The head of the new college, André de Gouveia, had been principal at the College of Guiene in Bordeaux. His students there included both Montaigne, who described him as 'the greatest principal in France', and Ignatius Loyola. But Coimbra was soon suspected of Calvinist contamination (the presence on its staff of the Scottish scholar George Buchanan lends some credibility to the accusations) and, after attention from the Inquisition, was handed over to the Jesuits in 1558.

Luis Vaz de Camões grew up during this period. It is generally accepted that he was born in 1524, probably in Lisbon. The Camões family belonged to the minor nobility and was relatively poor but well-connected. He was around twelve when the Inquisition was established and must have been studying at Coimbra, (if he did attend a university, as his extraordinary erudition seems to suggest), when the first *auto-da-fé* took place in the early 1540s. Camões' early years are largely guesswork, but there is no doubt that he spent much of his turbulent youth in the streets of Lisbon.

Lisbon, the gateway for Europe's trade with the

Orient, was a city in which everything could be bought and sold: spices, jewels, slaves, sex, drugs, power, fortunes, voyages, nobility, sanctity. In a verse epistle addressed to King John III, the humanist poet Sá de Miranda adapted Horatian pastoral to the situation of Portugal, portraying greed as the worst form of servitude and warning that the chief danger was not the aggression of Castile but Lisbon itself, where 'at the scent of cinnamon' the kingdom was being drained of its populace, while the 'bright poison' coming into the city was 'putting some of its citizens to sleep, others to death, and filling the streets with dreamers'.

In these contaminated streets the young Camões joined bohemian circles, keeping dubious company and frequenting brothels. Either 'at the scent of cinnamon' or in search of military honours as a means to improve his poor financial prospects, he served as a soldier in Ceuta, and it is generally assumed that it was there in a skirmish with the Moors that he lost an eye. He was soon back in Lisbon, where his bohemian life seems not to have precluded frequent attendance at court. He participated in courtly poetical debates and, according to tradition, seduced one (or more) of the kingdom's most noble ladies. His friends at court must have stood him in good stead when, in 1552, he was imprisoned as one of a gang charged with mugging a palace official. He secured a royal pardon on the understanding that he was 'an impoverished young man' who would be going to serve in India. He left for India in 1553 as a simple soldier, not in a spirit of heroic adventure but in protected exile. Sixteen years were to pass before he returned.

The four extant letters written by Camões – one from Ceuta, two from Lisbon and one from Goa – provide us with a picture of his life in Lisbon, the intrigues, street brawls and sexual adventures, an essential expression of his exuberant personality. In one letter he describes how the death of a useful 'madam' (murdered by her husband) led a group of frightened 'ladies' with 'young faces and old pipes' to seek refuge in a strong 'tower of Babel', where 'so many languages are already spoken that it is bound to fall soon, for there you will see Moors, Jews, Castilians, Leonese, friars, clerics, married men, bachelors, youths and old men'. In another letter, after mentioning a number of muggings of common friends, he warns the addressee that 'a warrant has been issued in this country to arrest some eighteen of us' on suspicion that they had beaten up a nobleman on the night of St. John. In the letter written from Goa, which he describes in what has become a cliché as 'mother of villains and stepmother of honest men', he nostalgically compares the 'pickled flesh' of the local prostitutes (overripe Portuguese and naive natives) with the irresistible 'coquetries' of the Lisbon 'ladies' who 'squeak like new pitchers filled with water'. He promises to receive them in Goa 'with all due pomp and circumstance' if they 'brave the discomforts of six months at sea', for if to the Goan prostitutes 'you try to speak of love in the words of Petrarch or Boscan they will reply in speech larded with straw, which sticks in the gullet of understanding and pours cold water on the most fiery enthusiasm'.

During his first three years in India, Camões completed his compulsory military service, taking part in expeditions to the Malabar coast and the Red Sea. Later, he seems to have alternated unemployment with occasional appointments to government posts. It is certain that he held the office of 'trustee for the property of the dead and absent' in Macao, but lost any wealth he amassed when the ship taking him back to India was wrecked at the mouth of the river Mekong. According to his account he managed to swim to shore with the manuscript of *Os Lusiadas*, the epic poem he had been writing for years. Tradition has it that his Chinese mistress died in the shipwreck. Shortly after his arrival Goa he was imprisoned for allegedly embezzling funds entrusted to him in Macao. Having lost everything in the shipwreck he was unable to make restitution and his life of poverty and exile continued. Around 1568 an influential friend helped him to travel from Goa to Mozambique. There, after quarrelling with his protector – the holder of the Mozambique captaincy – he was found living in dire poverty by some old friends, including the chronicler Diogo do Couto, the main source for this episode in Camões' life. His friends paid his debts and shared the cost of his return to Lisbon in 1569.

According to Couto, an important part of Camões' lyric verse was stolen from him during his sojourn in Mozambique. Even so, his vast extant works show how central poetry was to his life. In addition to the 1102 stanzas of *Os Lusiadas* and three plays, Camões' work comprises some 350 poems – a number of doubtful attribution: roundels, sonnets, eclogues, odes, octaves, elegies, canzones and a sestina.

After *Os Lusiadas* was published in 1572, this uncomfortable outsider's reputation began to spread. Tasso called him the 'prince of poets' in a sonnet – high praise from the other major epic poet of the time. But Camões' personal fortune did not improve much. Sebastian, the young king to whom he dedicated his epic, was educated in an atmosphere of fanaticism with few traces of the humanism Camões had known at court. Sebastian granted him a pension which, though modest, would have proved adequate had it not been for its irregular payment and the poet's incapacity, even as he approached old age, to mend his spendthrift ways. In 1578 Sebastian died in a foolhardy military expedition to North Africa. The flower of the Portuguese nobility died with him. Two years later the crown was annexed by Sebastian's uncle, Philip II of Spain who, on entering Portugal, is said to have asked to see Camões. But the poet had died on 10 June that year, victim of an outbreak of plague regarded by his superstitious countrymen as a sign of the ending of Portugal's golden age.

The first biography of Camões was published thirty-three years after his death. Others followed in 1624 and 1639. These seventeenth century biographical reconstructions include romanticized conjectures which were heavily embroidered over the next 300 years. Diogo do Couto's contemporary account of his meeting with the poet in Mozambique was only published posthumously and may well include apocryphal interpolations. Even so, the character evoked by these sources corresponds to the few facts actually known about Camões. Diogo do Couto describes him as 'a man with a terrible nature' and Pedro de Mariz, his first biographer (1613) portrays him as 'a great spender, liberal and magnificent, whose worldly goods remained in his possession only so long as he did not find occasion to spend them as he pleased'. When he was buried, years after his death (when it was no longer possible to determine for certain which of the many corpses in the plague pit was that of Camões) the inscription on his tombstone read: 'Here lies Luis de Camões, prince of the poets of his age. He lived as he died, miserably and in poverty'.

And what did he look like? Manuel Severim de Faria wrote 44 years after the poet's death: 'Luis de Camões was of middling height, thickset and full-faced. He had a long nose, tilting upwards in the middle and thick at the end; his looks were much spoiled by the loss of his right eye in youth. His hair was so fair as to be almost saffron-coloured; his appearance was not graceful but he was a fluent conversationalist, lively and witty . . . although as he grew older he became somewhat melancholy. He never married and had no issue.'

Writers on Camões have found it difficult to reconcile the personality of the man with the greatness of the poet. They tend to minimize his 'peccadillos' or to turn his misfortunes into the consequences of unjust persecutions. The basic problem is to come to terms with Camões' novel and disturbing perspective on the world and how he tried to make it intelligible through his poetry.

Camões, like Dante or Petrarch (and like the Neo-Platonist poets who modelled themselves on these masters) saw love as the vehicle of knowledge. But each perceives the nature of this knowledge differently. While Dante and Petrarch sought to reveal an inherent spiritual order obscured by the material world, Camões sought to shape a new order reconciling spirit and matter, idea and experience, in the harmonious man which the Renaissance idealised.

The progress of this quest can be traced in his lyric poetry and, though the exact chronology of the poems is unknown, they can be divided in thematic and stylistic terms into three main phases. In the first, the poet assumes and displays the sexual urgency of a profane neophyte conducting an active campaign of conquest. He delights in demystifying Petrarchan conventions of love as vain hypocrisy. This is the case with the famous *vilancete* to Catarina, who 'promises but lies' and who is assured that great delights await her if she keeps her word. The tone is light but the sense is not unlike Marvell's admonishments to his Coy Mistress almost a century later. In another *vilancete* he makes use of metaphors of sea and ship to indulge in sexual innuendo, promising solid virility to the lady still hesitating to embark – less, it is implied, because she fears for her virtue than because she finds it difficult to choose from among various possible 'barques'. This unconventional acceptance of natural female sexual desire is also present in the *vilancete* in which, with an ironic sense of fetishism as inherent in courtly love as it was later in romantic love, Camões makes the lady complain that her lover seems more attracted to her bonnet than her body which, 'like love', should be 'naked'.

These themes are transmuted in poems of greater philosophical weight such as the sonnets and canzones, where they are integrated into the pattern of a painful and complex voyage into the unknown, in which personal experience becomes both the supreme criterion of judgement and the principal end. In the sonnet 'Enquanto quis Fortuna que tivesse' ('While it was Fortune's will that I should have') Camões warns that the various ways in which Love expresses itself in his verses are not 'defects' – as they would be regarded by the moral and poetic codes associated with Petrarchism – but 'pure truths' ('verdades puras') which readers may and should understand according to their own personal experience. Individual experience is seen as the touchstone for an aesthetic whose purity stems from the desire to explore the variety of human potential. Almost two centuries were to pass before the rationalist concept of the 'libertine' gave philosophical coherence to the dark areas Camões was probing.

Mapping this difficult course becomes the theme in the second phase of his lyric poetry. It finds expression in a sonnet which at once suggests his view of love as a guide to the unknown and the mission of the poet as an instrument of the collective quest he personifies:

Não canse o cego amor de me guiar
a parte donde não saiba tornar-me;
nem deixe o mundo todo de escutar-me,
enquanto me a voz fraca não deixar.

[May blind love never tire of guiding me/to parts from whence I know of no return;/and may the whole world never cease to hear me,/so long as I have a feeble voice to sing.]

In *Os Lusiadas* (that most ambiguous of epic poems, in which celebration of the heroic past serves as criticism of a present lived in a 'mean and vile sadness') the heroes are also guided by love to a place of no return. His Venus guides them. She combines the spiritual attributes of 'Aphrodite Urania', the spiritual Venus identified with the Christian Virgin, and the sensuality and licentiousness of 'Aphrodite Porne', or Venus the Harlot. It is this same Venus who transforms her dual nature into the Island of Love which she causes to emerge from the sea in order to 'restore the tired humanity' of the mariners at the end of their adventure, leading them to the divine revelation that transforms them into 'enlightened heroes'. This daring metaphor of the spiritualization of sexuality (transmuting the basically carnal encounter of sailors and prostitutes in any of the world's ports, or even his memory of the Lisbon brothels in which Petrarch was a subject of conversation) has perplexed Camões' critics, who prefer to concentrate on the patriotic visionary and moralist. But the metaphor is central to his work, even if the poetic quest for knowledge through love did not lead, in personal terms, to the consecration of universal harmony embodied in the heroes of *Os Lusiadas*.

In the last phase of his lyric poetry we find Camões snared in a world of chaos and confusion, where love, like a savage goddess, is not content with the symbolic sacrifice of 'lambs and calves' but demands the cruel reality of human sacrifice ('Em prisões baixas fui um tempo atado', 'In mean jails for a time I had to languish'). What he sees as the essence of an order where an 'unjust Fortune is more than errors deserved' is the unreason of the arbitrary and the accidental in a world 'so confused that it seems to be forgotten by God', a world in which 'life has no more in it than what it seems to have'. He realizes that life has lived him, making him 'lose what the loss of fear has taught' ('Que poderei do mundo já querer', translated as 'What have I still to ask from the world's store'). As an epitaph for his project to transform the accidental course of life into rational and intelligible discourse, he writes 'Errei todo o discurso de meus anos' – 'I have mistaken all the discourse of my years', with the ambiguity of 'mistake' or 'error' as both 'fail' and 'wander', and 'discourse' as both 'speech' and 'trajectory', condensing in this line the complexity of his poetic and existential pilgrimage ('Erros meus, má Fortuna, amor ardente'- 'Errors of mine, misfortune, fires of love').

What Camões regarded in his blackest moments as the failure of his life's project – the discourse which could transform appetite into reason, and reason into knowledge, through love – finds its most negative expression in the Christian Platonism of the poem 'Babel e Siao' ('By the rivers of Babylon') inspired by Psalm 137. Here Camões submits to puritanical values, prostrating himself before an avenging Christ and renouncing his secular work. Many critics consider this the most sublime moment in his poetry, a judgement which may reveal as much about the attitudes of critics as about the spiritual solution they attribute to Camões. This despairing poem is important, however, if only because it focuses the element of metaphysical risk inherent in the quest recorded in the body of his work. In any event, the exact date of the poem is not known, though it is probable that it was written during his time in exile – according to some sources after his shipwreck, according to others during his bleak sojourn in Mozambique – rather than during his later years in Lisbon, where he supposedly came under the influence of the Dominicans.

One of his last compositions was a poem in heroic octaves, addressed to the Cardinal-Prince Henry, interceding on behalf of a married woman who had committed adultery during her husband's absence and was facing deportation to India. The poem lacks the metaphysical resonance that gives 'Babel e Sião' its unique place among Camões works, but its appeal for compassion suggests that he did not sacrifice his understanding of human frailty on the altar of righteousness.

Selected Poems

CONTENTS

The asterisks indicate titles or dedications given by Camões

Ao Leitor

Enquanto quis Fortuna que tivesse
Esperança de algum contentamento,
O gosto de um suave pensamento
Me fez que seus efeitos escrevesse.

Porém, temendo Amor que aviso desse
Minha escritura a algum juízo isento,
Escureceu-me o engenho co tormento,
Para que seus enganos não dissesse.

Ó vós que Amor obriga a ser sujeitos
A diversas vontades! Quando lerdes
Num breve livro casos tão diversos,

Verdades puras são, e não defeitos . . .
E sabei que, segundo o amor tiverdes,
Tereis o entendimento de meus versos!

To the Reader

While it was Fortune's will that I should have
Some prospect of the happiness I sought
I found that the delight of a sweet thought
Moved me to write of the results it gave.

But Love then, fearful that what I might say
Were earnest of an independent mind
With torment turned my wits, made fancy blind
So that I would not give his game away.

O you enslaved to Love, whom he subjects
To divers whims! When in one short book you
Shall read of consequences so diverse

They are plain truths I tell, and not defects . . .
And know that by such love as you have, so
You will have understanding of my verse!

Leonor

Barefoot to the fountain goes
Leonor where goats are tended —
Beautiful and undefended.

On her head she bears the pot
In her silver hands the lid
Her waist with fine scarlet wound
And her breast in camlet hid;
Her plain kirtle beats the snows —
It so spotless, she so splendid
Beautiful and undefended.

Bonnets do not cover throats
Nor do crimson ribbons twirled
Round such golden hair conceal;
Such looks so amaze the world
That it rains down grace that flows
And with beauty soon is blended
Beautiful and undefended.

On Her Beauty

Nature from her varieties of grace
Made a fair treasure that cannot be sold:
With rubies and with roses, snow and gold
She shaped a lofty, angelic loveliness —

On the mouth set the rubies, on the pure
Fair face the roses which for me are fatal
Upon the hair the wealth of golden metal
Upon the breast the snow which kindles fire

But on the eyes she showed what she could do
Making of them a sun where light more bright
Than brightest day is proved both pure and true

And then, Lady, in all of you complete
She finally could prove how much she knew
Of gold, of roses, rubies, snow and light.

Surrender

All that I am and have
Take as your due
But leave me with my eyes
To look at you.

All in this body is
Your residue:
When you have seized its life
Seize its death too.

If I have more to lose
Distrain it, do
But leave me with my eyes
To look at you.

The Sling

I put my eyes in a sling
Shot them high and heard them ring
On the bars of a window.

A young lady naughtily
Took her own eyes in her hand
Aimed the handful straight at me
Hit my heart, I felt it land:
I put my eyes in the sling
Shot and waited for the ring
But crash! I broke her window.

Love

Love is a fire that burns but is not seen
It is a wound that hurts but is not felt
It is a deal of joy that is not dealt
It is a woe that maddens with no pain

A wish for nothing but that wish expressed
A walking solitary through the crowd
A joy with all enjoyment disallowed
A care increasing as it runs to waste

It is a longing to be held in thrall
The victor vanquished, laying down his arms
To serve one who leads honour to a fall

But how come that its favour can bring charms
To take possession of the hearts of all
If love so promptly contradicts its terms?

Jacob and Rachel

Seven long years as shepherd Jacob slaved
For Laban, Rachel the fair lass's father:
It was not him he served, but Rachel rather
And she alone was all the prize he craved.

He spent the days when he could only see her
In hope of one day that he would enjoy:
Meanwhile her father by a wicked ploy
Instead of Rachel landed him with Leah.

The shepherd, seeing on the point of tears
That he'd been tricked out of his shepherdess
As if he had not worked for her enough

Sets out to serve another seven years
Saying: I would have served still more than this
But life's too short for such a length of love!

The Boat

Who tells you my boat lies
Sister, is telling lies.

You want to take a ride?
You long to have away?
Come aboard, why delay!
Look, now it is high tide!
What sailor by your side
Tells you that this boat lies
Sister, is telling lies!

This boat is at a stand
All newly fitted out:
There is no boat about
So ready to command.
If, to take you in hand
One tells you that it lies
Sister, he's telling lies!

61

Kate

*Kate promises the skies
But damn it, how she lies!*

Kate is as fair as day
Though I rate her the higher;
But fairer still she'd be
If she were not a liar.
Today she's nice enough;
Tomorrow otherwise
So I suspect she lies.

Kate has told lies to me
So often, none could save her
But for one truth she told
I willingly forgave her.
She spoke to me, and if
She speaks more, in my eyes
She'll never more tell lies.

You evil, wicked girl
I said, why are you lying?
You promise, then you quit
And all my hopes are dying.
For you don't know your brief:
Who promises and lies
Heaves at his loss no sighs.

That bitch swore she would come
By the soul that she cherished.
She tricked me; she has mine:
She'd not care if it perished.
For her I spend my life:
She promises, I rise
But I sink when she lies.

To your desire would fall
Every last thing you wanted
If your promise that I
Would come were to be granted.
Then we would have all off:
You whom life satisfies
Would laugh at one who lies.

She promised yesterday
To come: she did not make it.
I think she made a vow
Just so that she could break it.
She makes me weep and laugh:
I laugh when 'yes' she cries
I weep when 'yes' she lies.

But since you leave your lies
And promise me a meeting
Promise away, and leave
The rest to my completing:
Then you will know enough
Who's happier – who lies
Satisfied, or who lies.

Partridge

Partridge has lost his pen:
He'll never smile again.

Partridge, whose plumy mind
Raised him above his station,
Instead of elevation
Has pain, not pen, behind.
In neither air nor wind
Will plumeless wings sustain:
He'll never smile again.

So high he sought to fly
But found himself unplumed:
Unpenned he now is doomed
In pain he soon will die.
Stoke up! Let the sparks fly
For he complains in vain:
He'll never smile again.

Outwitted by Love

Let Love seek out new arts, new artfulness
To kill me, for he cannot with old dodges
Draw away any hope from where none lodges
Nor may he steal what I do not possess.

Behold what hope I hoard for my upkeep
And see how dangerous my confidence!
For I fear no reverses, change nor chance
Being all at sea, having abandoned ship.

But though a man cannot be disappointed
Who has no hope, Love with one woe lurks there
That kills though it is hidden from the eye

For there are days when all my soul is haunted
By who knows what, that springs from who knows where
Comes who knows how, and hurts me who knows why.

The Wimple

A muslin wimple
Has stolen simple
Simon's heart away.

So you're in love
With nothing rarer?
You love the hair
But not the wearer?
My wits waste away
For you, but simple
Simon loves a wimple.

You love my clothes?
You're a false lover.
Don't you see Love
Prefers no cover?
I'm yours till doomsday
But you, my simple
Simon, love a wimple.

Let him who sees
Say in good season
You're leaving me
For no good reason!
You can laugh away.
My heart breaks: simple
Simon loves a wimple.

She who loves thus
Deserves some loving
But all I feel
Is your hand shoving.
Look, 'tis clear as day:
Love just me, simple
Simon, leave the wimple.

Everyone finds
Your nonsense shocking.
Gonzalo sings
This song of mocking:
A muslin wimple
Has stolen simple
Simon's heart away.

Here in my hair
I don't know what you
Saw that Love seized
His bow and shot you.
Don't get in a way:
Just love me, simple
Simon, leave the wimple.

(Poor Simon groaned
And Mary wept for
All the heartache
She had not slept for:
And she tore away
Her tears, not simple
Simon's fatal wimple.)

I don't know why
Your love needs clothing:
Cupid himself
Goes dressed in nothing.
So why the wimple?
The answer's simple:
Simon likes it that way.

64

On the Death of Dona Maria De Távora*

Cruel Death, what's that you carry? 'A bright day.'
At what hour did you come for it? 'At dawn.'
What knowledge have you of your burden? 'None.'
Who has, then? 'He who bids me bear away.'

Who now enjoys her body? 'The cold earth.'
How was it with her light? ''Twas growing dark.'
And Portugal? 'It cannot but remark:
Dona Maria was of greater worth.'

You killed who saw her die? 'There was no need.'
What has harsh Love to say? 'He dare not speak.'
Who bids him hold his tongue? 'It is my will.'

And at court, what is left? 'High hearts that bleed.'
What is there still to see? 'To see these break:
Her beauty leaves a void no tears can fill.'

The Reproach

False ungrateful knight, what say you
To betray me?
You say I slay you
And you slay me.

'Tis an old trick to betray
Innocence —
A grave countenance
But a heart that will away.
I love you, and you, false lover,
Make me suffer:
You say I slay you
And you slay me.

Who is now in a worse way
Who is dying?
Enough of your lying
For you are at fault, they say.
When I moan that you misuse me
You accuse me
Of hate to slay you
And you slay me.

Mutability

Times change with seasons, men too change their mind
We change the way we are, the way we feel:
Everyone, everything is changeable
Made to take on the new in every kind.

The new confronts our vision without let
All is different, unexpected all:
Of ill it is the sorrow we recall,
Of good, if there was any, the regret.

For time covers the ground with a green cloak
That was but lately covered with cold snow
And turns my sweet song to a mournful croak.

Beyond this daily changing there is too
A change that fills us with a greater shock —
That nothing changes as it used to do.

66

Swansong

The morning crimson-bright
Has flung wide all the portals of the east
   And from the hills released
The black gloom that is envious of light.
   The sun without respite
Impatient to behold her merry face
   Pursues impetuous
Driving his team of travail-weary horses
That sniff the cool fresh dew upon the grasses
And stretches merry, bright and luminous.
   The small birds as they fly
Tuning from branch to branch their melody
With music soft and sweet upon the ear
Gaily declare
                    the brightness of the day.

Letting her face be seen
The fair and gentle morning bids the groves
    Cover themselves with leaves
So mild, so soft, so angelic, so serene.
    Alas, delicious pain!
O most illustrious effect of love
    To sanction and approve
That wheresoever I may chance to be
Her look of seraph I may always see
For which I am content to live and grieve!
    But you could not care less
Pure Dawn, what from your treasury you bless
For such variety you have tucked away
Thus to portray
                such various loveliness.

    The soft and cheerful light
Shows my eyes her for whose sake I despair
    Nor can its golden hair
Match what I saw, but only imitate.
    This is what puts to flight
The black gloom of the hours wherein I brood
    And brings a sweeter mood;
The dew that on the fragile flowers lies
Is all those weary tears that from my eyes
For pleasure in my torment fall in flood;
    The small birds that rejoice
Are all my spirits lifting up their voice
Declaring me a pilgrim, till they astound
The world around
                with such a heavenly noise.

    As one who lives in fear
While danger looms to take dear life away
    And he prepares to die,
To him some holy vision will appear
    So to me, drained of cheer
In life, which is, my Lady, you alone
    To this soul which you own

While it is parted from its rightful prison
At the same time be you revealed and risen
Appearing as the lovely crimson dawn!
    O happy separation!
O sovereign glory, airy elevation —
If my desire should not deny it me!
For what I see
                points me to my salvation.

    Nature nevertheless
That showed herself thus pure until this last
    Now fails me quite as fast
As now the swift sun fails the earth's fair face.
    Should you call feebleness
To die in such dejection and despair
    The blame is Love's to bear
Or yours, the host of his distracted heart
For you caused him to dwell so long apart
That he might lose his life with all his care.
    For if I cannot live
(A mere man – flesh and bones are all I leave)
This life I lose now, Love it was that gave it:
I cannot save it —
                death is yours to give.

A swansong, fashioned in my final hour.
    The cold hard masonry
Of memory is yours, for company
The chiselled lettering upon my tomb:
Even now its gloom
                is shutting out my day.

Departure

That daybreak full of gloom and gaiety
With woe and sympathy quite overset —
As long as in the world there is regret
I want it called to mind perpetually.

It alone when delectably enamelled
It came forth and the world with light provided
Saw itself from another will divided
That cannot see its own self but entrammelled.

It alone saw the tears join in a seam
Confluent, sprung from these and other eyes
To swell into a great and sprawling stream

And it saw all the words instinct with cries
Which would have turned away the loveless flame
And comforted each damned soul where it dies.

The Paradox

Moment by moment I am drained of life —
If it is true perchance that still I live:
Fleet-footed time runs from before my eyes
I shed tears for the past, and when I speak
The days are stepping past me step by step.
I lose the years and I am left with pain.

And O how harsh the manner of this pain
Since never from its woe such a long life
Has seen one hour in which it might shift step!
What do I care now that I die or live?
Why do I weep, in short? Why do I speak
If I can have no pleasure from my eyes?

O beautiful, O lovely limpid eyes
Whose absence moves my heart to so much pain
I cannot comprehend it as I speak!
If at the end of such a long, brief life
You should inflame me, you who brightly live
Then I would cherish each and every step.

But well I know that first my final step
Must be to come and close my tearful eyes
That Love may show me those for which I live.
They will be witnesses, this pen, this pain:
They will set down of such a tiresome life
How little I have spent, how much I speak.

I know not what I write, nor what I speak!
And if from one thought to the next I step
I behold such a wretched kind of life
That if it shall hold cheap so many eyes
I cannot fancy what may be the pain
Fit to displace this pain with which I live.

Constant within my soul flames leap and live
Which if they did not breathe through what I speak
Would have become by now ashes and pain:

Exile

Here in this Babylon where enough raw ill
Springs to supply the needs of the whole earth
Here where pure Love has forfeited his worth
To his more powerful mother who soils all

Here where ill is refined and good is blamed
And tyranny has seized the upper hand
From honour, here where kingship wandering blind
Takes care that reputations are defamed

Here in this labyrinth where nobility
Panting and knowledge cap in hand must come
Before the gates of greed and villainy

Here in this murky pandemonium
The law of the jungle rules: ah, woe is me
If I forget you, O Jerusalem!

But as the greater grief quickens its step
Tears temper me by streaming from my eyes
Which do not put an end to fleeting life.

Dying I cling to life,
                in death I live.
I see without eyes,
                without tongue I speak.
I keep in step
        with glory and with pain.

To A Captive He Fell In Love With In India Called Barbara*

That fair prisoner
Who holds me captive
Wants only to live
For I live in her.
I never saw rose
In a sweet bouquet
That was more shapely
Than she in my eyes.

All the stars above
All the flowers below
Are possessed of no
Beauty like my love:
Her face is thrilling
Her calm eyes are deep
Black and full of sleep
But not from killing

And they are alive
With a grace ready
To make a lady
Out of a captive
Black also her hair
Where vain folk question
Their opinion
That laurels are fair.

Blackness, I love you
Whose form is so smooth
The snow swears an oath
That it will change hue!
Gentle ways that go
Gaily with good sense
Suggest innocence
But a savage — no!

Serene presence, best
Balm for the wild main!
Therein all my pain
Finally finds rest.
She's the prisoner
Who holds me captive
She is strength to live
Since I live in her.

70

The Pursuit

O how from year to year they reach and stretch —
My endless, friendless, weary wanderings!
And how it shrinks toward the end of things —
This verse, my vain, shortwinded human speech!

Age wastes away and losses multiply;
A remedy I had begins to go;
If from experience I seek to know
Any great hope I kept is a great lie.

I chase this good but never catch it once:
It fails me in the middle of the way;
A thousand times I fall, lose confidence.

It flees, I dally, and in dalliance
If I look up to see how far away
It is, I lose of it both sight and chance.

Arabia Felix

Hard by a parched, a wild, a barren mountain
Useless and bare with bald and shapeless steeps
A vacuum that nature has abhorred
Where not a bird flies, not a wild beast sleeps
Nor is clear flowing stream nor bubbling fountain
Nor verdant bough with softly warbling bird;
Whose name the common people have conferred
Is apt only by opposition — Felix;
　　Which nature turned away
　　And planted on the side
Where, stretching out an arm, the seas divide
From Arab harshness Abyssinia
Where Berenice now is merely relics
　　Once built on that side where

The sun that boils within deflects its glare;

Therein appears the cape with which the coast
Of Africa that runs up from the south
Is rounded off, Aromata by name.
Aromata no more; for the uncouth
Tongue of the natives as the moons have passed
Has licked away all trace of the old perfume.
Here on a sea impetuous to come
In through the throat of this arm where tides race
　　I am brought by my hard luck
　　And detained for a time.
Here in this far away, this harsh, this grim
Part of the world it wanted life to brook
For all its brevity this one brief space
　　That my life might be shattered
And all its fragments round the world left scattered.

Here I have sampled many days of ill
Days of hard labour, woeful days and lonely
Arduous days that make me rage and moan;
Holding as enemies to life not only
The white heat of the sun, the waters' chill,
Fat, eager faces meeting with my frown;
But my own broodings too, which are my own
To cheat Nature herself, make her my foe
　　Have been confronting me
　　And bringing to my mind
Some short-lived glory I have left behind
Who saw it in the world in my heyday
To swell twofold the harshness of my woe
　　To show me that I spent
In the world many hours of merriment.

Here with these broodings fate bade me remain
Sampling the days, the life; which lifted me
So high upon their pinions that I dropped
(And see how slight the somersault would be!)
From happiness of which I dreamed in vain

Into a loss of all for which I hoped . . .
Here expectations toppled, here they sloped
Straight down to tears and sighs from broken hearts
   No longer debonair.
   Here my afflicted soul
All wounded lay, its fleshly prison whole
Though set about with sorrow and with care
Abandoned and uncovered to the darts
   Of Fortune, her the proud
Whose will takes no rebuke, whose voice is loud.

Nowhere I had to settle down secure
Nor was there any hope of leaning over
My head a little for a moment's rest:
All things to it are grief and cause to suffer
But not to perish, that it might endure
Destiny's evermore untamed behest.
O how I tame this angry, screaming waste
Of waters! And these winds' relentless howling
   Seems to be holding back!
   Only unbending heaven,
The stars and fate which none will ever govern
Amuse themselves with my perpetual wreck
Showing themselves all-powerful and scowling
   Against a lump of earth
A lowly crawling worm so little worth.

If I might but redeem from all these tears
The certain knowledge still that some short hour
Flashed back to eyes that used to flash at me
And if this sad voice with a sudden roar
Might register in those angelic ears
Of her in whose sweet laugh was my heyday;
Who, turning from herself somewhat away
To ruminate though ever in a hurry
   On the times long since spent
   Of my tender mistakes
Of my impassioned rages, my sweet aches
Suffered, sought after, all on her account —

Who, turning (rather late it might be) sorry
   Might weigh somewhat in mind
And to herself judge that she was unkind;

Might I know only this, my mind would be
At rest throughout the life left to me here;
I would embrace my anguish knowing this.
Ah, Lady, Lady! For you are so dear
That at this far remove you nourish me
With a fair fantasy of happiness
And as my brooding fixes on your face
I banish all my trouble, all my pain.
   Only with thoughts of you
   Do I find strength and faith
Against the fearsome features of wild Death
And then hopes gather for my retinue
With which my brow as it turns more serene
   Finds its grim torments turning
Into a sweet regret, a gentle yearning.

Here, left with them I labour to find out
From the caressing winds that softly blow
Some news of you, Lady, from where you are
From the birds flying there, had they seen you
What were you doing, talking what about
And where, and how, with whom, what day, what hour.
There, weariness of life has found a cure
And takes new spirits that it may lay low
   Fortune and Trouble, just
   To return to your sight
Enter your service and your love's delight.
Time tells me it trims all, makes nothing last
But hot desire, that never will allow
   Any delay, unheeding
Opens my wounds afresh and sets them bleeding.

Such is my life; if anyone should ask you
   Song, how I do not die
Tell him that it is just because I die.

The New Circe

A gentle, gracious movement of the eyes
On nothing fixed, a gentle, open smile
Forced almost, an expression without guile
That when joy beckons holds back, humbly wise

A quiet and reserved self-confidence
A spirit shy and serious, at rest
A simple goodness making manifest
A soul free of all dullness and pretence

A boldness within bounds, a gentleness
A guiltless fear, an air of no commotion
A tolerance obedient and kind:

This was for me the heavenly loveliness
Of a new Circe, this the magic potion
Whose drug has power to transform my mind.

The Transformation

The lover changes into what he loves
Through force of fancy that may so inspire:
My sole possession, then, is my desire
For its dear object deep within me moves.

If into that my soul is changed, what goal
Remains to be desired by flesh and bone?
It can find rest within itself alone
There being no other bond for such a soul.

But now this demigoddess, fair and clear
Who like an outward feature of her slave
Thus with my soul establishes her norm

Exists within my thought as pure idea
And the quick clear love which I am and have
Like inner substance labours toward form.

On Her Death

What have I still to ask from the world's store?
For where I have invested love so great
I have seen nothing but displeasure, hate
And death, just now — so there can be no more!

Since life has no contentment still to bring
Since now I know that great grief does not kill
If anything affords a greater ill
I shall see it, who can see everything.

With death to weigh me down I am guaranteed
Full weight of all my woes, and I have lost
Whatever taught me once to lose my dread.

In life it is hatred I have seen at most
In death the great grief I shall never shed:
Only for this, it seems, was my lot cast!

To His Beloved In Heaven

O noble soul I love, who bade farewell
So fast to this life you were loth to leave
Rest there in heaven always, let me live
Here upon earth for ever sorrowful.

If there where you have risen, in the skies
A memory of this life is allowed
Do not forget that burning love which glowed
As pure as once you saw it in my eyes.

And should you see that some small merit there
May be obtained from all the woe that stays
From when your loss first choked me with despair

Ask God, O ask him who cut short your days
To lift me to your sight as fast from here
As then he lifted you beyond my gaze.

The Dream

When the long brooding on my misery
Draws sleep across my eyes still wet with tears
In dreams that lovely soul once more appears
Who in this life was but a dream to me.

There in a lonely place, a broad flat field
The sight of which, as I behold it, dims
I run towards her; whereupon she seems
To slip yet further from me, as though compelled.

I shout: 'Don't run away from me, kind shade!'
But she, her eyes upon me sweetly shy
As if to say that now it cannot be

Turns, flees. 'Dyna. . . ,' I scream. I have not said
'. . . mene' before I start awake, and why? —
Not even a brief delusion is for me.

Nocturnal

The sky, the earth, the wind subdued and quiet.
The waves that ripple shoreward from the deep.
The fishes in the sea becalmed in sleep.
The soft reposeful silence of the night.

The fisherman of Helicon who, sprawled
Where in the wind the water ebbs and bobs
Calls the beloved name in vain and sobs
For it can not be any more than called.

'O waves,' he said, 'before I am killed by love
Restore to me my nymph, whom you have taken
So early from me and enslaved to death.'

Nobody speaks to him. The sea far off
Slaps. In the wind the grove is gently shaken.
His voice is lifted, borne off on its breath.

By The Rivers Of Babylon*

Beside the rivers that stream
Through Babylon, there I stepped
And there I sat down and wept
Recalling Jerusalem
And the company I kept.
There I felt the rivers flow
From my eyes profuse and fast
And I likened first to last —
Babylon to present woe
Jerusalem to time past.

Memories of happiness
Paraded within my soul
And the things which now I miss
Stood forth with such emphasis
As if they were with me still.
There, as soon as I awoke
With tears streaming down my face
And the web of this dream broke
I saw pleasures that I took
Come to grief instead of grace

And I saw that all the tears
Spring from changes, that one weeps
For the changes wrought by years
Whence I saw how many dupes
Are what time makes out of hopes.
There I saw how little time
Even the greatest good thing lasts
And how quickly troubles come
And how sad the state of him
Who in fickle fortune trusts.

I saw that what we love well
Grows more precious when the course
Of joy suffers a reverse:
I saw good give rise to ill

And ill go from bad to worse.
And I saw what agony
Man must suffer to repent:
I saw nobody content
And I see myself, how my
Sad words on the wind are spent.

Torrents these tears are that flow
And upon this paper stream
And cruel indeed must seem
These varieties of woe —
Babel's pandemonium.
As a man who, let us say
For the troubles that befall
Since he turned from battle's call
Takes his weapons from the fray
Hangs them on the temple wall —

So, seeing the ravages
Time wreaks upon everything
For the woe that dogged my days
I hung on the willow trees
The harp to which I had sung.
I left that gay instrument
From the life I no more live
With these words: Music, my love
You shall be the monument
I leave in this sacred grove.

My flute which when played upon
Moved the mountains from their place
Through the ripples you would run
And the waters purling down
Would their liquid steps retrace
Nevermore will tigers stop
In their bloody tracks to hear
And the ewes at pasture there
Would for once forget to crop
Leave the grass to lend an ear.

No more will you sweetly make
The thorn turn into a rose
In the riverbank's green brake
Nor the current will you check —
Least if from my eyes it flows.

To move thickets 'tis too late
Nor behind you can you leave
The pure spring bubbling in spate
Because you could not remove
The reverses dealt by fate.

You are to be left behind
Pledged to ever watchful fame
Flute of which I am so fond
For with life never the same
Joys are ever redefined.
Youth in its tenderness goes
For those pleasures fit for it
But when riper years would choose
They will soon consider those
Former joys inadequate.

A joy that delights today
Tomorrow is seen no more:
Thus change sweeps us on its way
From hope to hope without stay
On from desire to desire.
And yet in a life so mean
What hope will continue strong?
To men all frailties belong:
Life has moments, in between
Death is clacking out its song!

But to leave before too late
In all this a song of youth!
Let no future care to state
'Tis of one long in the tooth
Or a work decreed by fate:
Whether age or time or fear
Seeing these last but a season
It would be beyond their power
While, if the song still be here
Still here too would be the reason.

But among my tears and sighs
In joy or on pleasure bent
Whether sun, snow, wind be sent
I shall keep before my eyes
Her for whom I die content.
Harp and flute I left behind
(Such dear spoils of victory)
On the willow in that land
And as trophy they remained
For her who had conquered me.

But memories of love's flame
That kept me a captive there
Demanded of me the same
Music then, to sing an air
I sang in Jerusalem.
What was it of that song, why
Should its short-lived praises last?
And why did I let it lie?
For it still serves to pass by
Some toil that is long since past.

The merry wayfarer sings
As through groves he toils his way
Full of wild imaginings
And by night the bold can stay
With song fears the darkness brings.
Sweetly sings the prisoner
As he fingers the hard chains
Sings too the glad harvester
And the toiler by his strains
Feels his toiling less severe.

I who have felt such a thing
In my soul full of despond
Have replied: How can you bring
A self that feels strange, to sing
A sweet song in a strange land?
How indeed can anyone

Who with his tears bathes his breast?
For whereas a toiling man
Sings to hold weariness down
Only I reject all rest

For no reason do I deem
Nor would good cause thereby hang
That, my passion's flood to stem
Here in Babylon I sang
The songs of Jerusalem
For when the great heaviness
Of regret turns to depress
This lively heart to the limit
That ere I die of distress
I should sing a song to stem it

For if thought's delicacy
Only in distress can lie
Torment holds no fear for me:
Would of mere distress to die
Not a greater gladness be?
Nor shall I sing on my flute
What I go through, have gone through
Nor yet thereof shall I write
For my pen will weary so
And my pain will not rest quiet

For if life so small and mean
Fills out in a foreign land
And if Love should so ordain
There is cause to tire my pen
Writing of a pain so grand.
Even so, if to display
Feelings that in the heart teem
Pen and pain shall weary me
Never may my memory
To fly to Jerusalem!

Blessed land most fortunate
If by any force whatever

From my soul you change estate
My pen may I dedicate
To forgetting you for ever
And this exile with its ache
Which I most want shaped in hard
Stone or iron none can break
May it never more be heard —
Punishing thus my mistake

And if singing be my whim
Here in Babylon oppressed
Far from you, Jerusalem
When my voice takes up a theme
Let it freeze within my breast.
Let my tongue cleave to the roof
Of my mouth after this loss
If as long as I live thus
In time I should cast you off
Damn you to forgetfulness!

But, O great and glorious land
If I never saw your essence
How do you recall my presence?
You only call me to mind
By a conscious reminiscence
For the soul is a blank page
That with divine doctrine writ
Can in its fancy take flight
Till it soars from its own cage
Homeward to the heavenly height.

It is therefore not regret
For the lands where life was given
To the flesh, it is for heaven
For that holy city, that
Land from which the soul was riven
And that form in human dress
Which can never here improve
Is not that for which to strive

But a ray of Loveliness
That alone deserves our love

For the eyes, the light which here
Kindle what keeps us subjected
(Not the sun's, but a lamp's fire)
Are but shade to that Idea
Which in God is best perfected
And what held me here in thrall
Are the affects whose strong feeling
Keeps our hearts subjected, kneeling:
Sophists were my teachers all
Whose strait paths have set me reeling!

These are the tyrants who rave
And require that I should whine
Braving the wrath from above
Rhapsodies of worldly love
Rather than some hymn divine
But I, lightened by the ray
Divine in a land where hard
Times and terrors mar my way
What have I to sing or say
That is only for the Lord?

Grace has such power to exalt
That it heals with kind correction
Commands life to change direction
And what I took for a fault
It made a step to perfection
And makes this natural love
Which we reckon such a prize
From shadow to substance move
From a single beauty rise
Towards that Beauty above.

So let it stay hanging there
That flute which thrilled with my tune
Jerusalem my desire
And let me take up the lyre

Of gold to hymn you alone
Not captive, dragging a chain
In this Babylon, this hell
But here, clear of every stain
And raised homeward to your plane
Both heavenly and natural

And if to this worldly show
Pressing, stern and unforgiving
My neck still I must be giving
Cancelled out be all I know
From the great book of the living
And as I take in my hand
The holy lyre, capable
Of a wit that shall transcend
Let this loud confusion end
And the vision of peace swell.

Let the world with terror fill
Let this holy accent ring —
Hear me, shepherd, listen, King:
Of all that I have sung ill
Now the palinode I sing.
By you only will I stand
Lord and Captain whose great power
Rules Jerusalem's high tower
To whose height without your hand
To raise me I cannot soar.

That great day, that hour sublime
When the lyre shall learnedly
Celebrate Jerusalem
Remember to deal your doom
To vile Edom's progeny.
Those who bearing the bloodstain
Of poor innocents still go
Proud in power that must be vain
Level all, and let them know
That they too are sons of men

And that ruthless might of all
Those affects with which I come
That set soul and wit aflame
Made a breach there in the wall
Of the free will I proclaim;
Those that in their fury swarm
Screaming as they come to scale me
Evil spirits full of harm
That want to take me by storm
And from my foundation fell me —

Fell them, let them skulk alone
Frail of nerve and faint of heart
For there is no way we can
Either with them to you run
Or without you from them part.
My own frailty will not do
To build my defences on
If, my Captain, holy one
Here within my fortress you
Do not post a garrison.

As for you, flesh with your charms
Daughter of Babel so foul
And of miseries so full
Who a thousand times take arms
Against him who takes control
Blessed only that man who
Can enlist celestial aid
To make a conquest of you
Who can come to you and do
The ill that to him you did;

He who with harsh discipline
Often deals himself the lash
And whose soul from vices clean
Lays upon his flesh a stain
As his soul was stained by flesh
And blessed is he to whom

It falls to take his devices
And at birth to smother them
Rather than see them become
Serious and pressing vices;

Who with them has buffeted
The stone of his holy rage
Whose blows have left them destroyed
On the stone which is the head
Of the corner in this age;
Who then, when his fancies twine
About evil flesh's throng
Of vice, will in thought incline
To that flesh which is divine
And upon the Cross was hung;

Who from the base happiness
Of this world of sight and sense
(As much as man can) shall hence
In understanding progress
To that of Intelligence
There he will discover joy
Perfect in all for his pleasure
Full of such soft harmony
That it does not with short measure
Delight, nor with surfeit cloy.

There on high he will behold
Such a depth of mystery
That, with nature vanquished, he
Will judge the pomps of the world
Vain for all their vanity.
Divine abode, happiest landing
My homeland unique and true
If but to imagine you
So exalts my understanding
What will my arrival do?

Happy he who shall depart
Bound for you, O splendid shore

Penitent enough to soar
Shriven to your shining heart
There to rest for evermore!

Towards Winter

Muddy they flow, the waters of this river
For those from heaven and the hills have muddied them;
Flowers of the field have withered on the stem;
The valley makes us turn away and shiver.

Gone is the spring, gone the hot summertime;
Some things to other things have shifted shape;
The treacherous Fates have long since given up
Ruling the world by statute or by whim.

Time has its order we already know
But not the world, whose riotous condition
Suggests that God has moved to other spheres.

Events, opinions, nature and tradition
Now lead us to regard this life as though
Nothing therein is more than what appears.

To His Genius

Errors of mine, misfortune, fires of love
Are locked in a conspiracy to damn me;
Errors there were and fortune fit to cram me
Though love alone would have been quite enough.

I have been through it all, yet great griefs press
Upon me so from what has long since been
That I have learned from sorrows and their spleen
To leave off the pursuit of happiness.

I have erred, I have strayed all down my years
And given Fortune good grounds to chastise
My hopes built on so little common sense.

Of love I have seen only tricks and tears . . .
O my harsh Genius! How much satisfies
Your lust to ply me so with punishments?

The Lesson

In mean jails for a time I had to languish —
A shameful punishment to purge my stains
And even now I walk dragging the chains
Which death has long since broken, to my anguish.

I sacrificed my life to what I wanted
For Love requires no slaughtered lamb or heifer
But grief, woe, exile have been mine to suffer:
It seems to me that fate has so appointed!

I was content with little, knowing well
That such contentment was a shameful thing —
Life pledged to the pursuit of appetite:

But now my star, at last predictable,
Blind death and doubt about what it may bring
Have taught me finally to dread delight.

Job's Curse

Let the day perish wherein I was born
Let time block off its course while ages run;
Never let it return, or let the sun
Suffer eclipse should ever it return.

Let the light fail it, let the sun be veiled
And let the world show forth signs of the end;
Let monsters breed, let blood like rain descend
And let the mother not know her own child.

Let men amazed in ignorance, with tears
Streaking their faces wan as though from grief
Think the world dashed as it had never been.

O people full of trembling, calm your fears
For to the world this day unfolded life
More miserable than was ever seen!

83

On The Disorder Of The World

To Dom António de Noronha

Who in the world can have such peace of mind
Or who will be so open in his thought
Who by experience so much refined
So free of snares in which most minds are caught
That either publicly or with his kind
His sense is not set reeling and distraught
Leaving his judgement out of kilter hurled
On noting the disorder of the world?

Who is there, seeing one who spent his time
In robberies, murders and adulteries
And who would be deemed worthy for such crime
Of pain for ever, great anathemas
If Fortune takes him up, advances him
(Showing in fact that all is mysteries)
Till he in triumph to eminence is raised —
Who then, however free, is not amazed?

Who is there, seeing one whose virtues stood
So shining that the very god of Blame
Judged him a paragon of rectitude
Though he had searched his inmost heart for shame
If evil Fortune, greedy but for good
Crushes him and denies his every claim —
Who then is in his own heart not left chilled
For all the experience with which it is filled?

Democritus once of the gods declared
There were two only — Pain and Benefit.
This must be some wild thing his fancy reared
For I find no clear evidence of it:
For if both come by some path unprepared
To who does not deserve them, it is a great
Vice in unjust, unreasonable gods.
Democritus, dream on: Paul never nods.

You'll tell me that if in the world again
This strange disorder caused me to reflect
Then I, the freest, cleverest of men
Should have no cause for shock, if I were shocked
But that if Socrates could once maintain
That no event whatever could affect
His face that ever wise and steadfast gazed
Then he might teach me not to be amazed.

That seems to be straight thinking, but I say
This attitude to Fortune does much harm
For the more seen as the accepted way
The more it is abused and warped in form
Because if heaven, so kindly in its sway
Does not allot to Fortune a fixed term
Then our amazement need not be so great
That evil should be so importunate.

Another, greater shock here puzzles me —
That, inasmuch as Fortune so profane
With these disorders keeps her mastery
She deceives no man, all can see her plain:
No man on hearing this philosophy
Of human life will not perceive it vain
And yet for all the insight he employs
Will claim at least a few of this world's joys.

Diogenes presumed to take his stand
On Plato's platform with his grubby feet
Showing with greater pride that he disdained
The pomp which men of this world cultivate.
Diogenes, look: they are far beyond
Whom you hound, sitting in your tub and state
For if you set such store by your disdain
The world must hold some prize you long to gain.

I leave aside now those great kings who wield
Their wits in honour of the greedy aim
To dominate, command and hold the field
With sheer extravagance and widespread fame

Lima de Freitas 1959

And I leave those who take up for a shield
To hide their vices and their lives of shame
The blue blood of their noble ancestors
Indifferent to better lives than theirs

And I leave him whose dreams make him a craver
Of great gifts from the king he so adores
Who on the air of false and fickle favour
Lives like so many hearts prone to its powers
And I leave those who pant and thirst and slaver
To stuff themselves with riches at all hours
Suffering from false dropsy, that complaint
Whereby the more they get the more they want

And I leave other follies that have fooled
Common folk who have none to say them nay
Who by no more authority are ruled
Than this opinion, that accepted way.
But now I summon Caesar brave and bold
Or Plato the divine, and bid them say —
This one, from all the lands where he has lain,
That one, from conquering them, what did he gain?

Caesar will say: 'My name deserves to carry
Who quelled all those bold peoples in my wars:
I ruled the world, and men will bear the story
Of my illustrious deeds to many shores.'
True, true: but that dominion, that glory —
Did you enjoy it long? Conspirators
Brutus and Cassius say so: you could win
The world, and then be murdered by your men.

Now Plato: 'To see Etna and the Nile
I went to Sicily, Egypt, other parts
Purely to see and write in a high style
Of natural science, using all my arts.'
Do you judge only labour worth your while
Plato, though time is short, giving your heart's
Devotion through those fleeting hours of study
To nothing better than a heavenly body?

Why is command worth more than being commanded
Why being simple more than being wise
If everything is by appointment ended
If everything is fixed by fate's decrees?
Command begets anxiety, suspended
Over the head of loyal Damocles
While out of wisdom, as the Preacher tells
Troubles increase and indignation swells.

For when out of its dark and earthly fetters
The soul from this world finds deliverance
It is preoccupied with such great matters
That fame is one of mere indifference.
Whether a lump of clay has feeling, let us
Consult the Cynic, in case he by chance
Upon the field where he was laid out dead
Set on by dogs and vultures kept his head!

He who so bridled his imagining
That with great things it never was concerned
Only with taking cows to the cool spring
And milking the great bounty he has earned —
To him what happiness his days would bring!
However much the wheel of Fortune turned
That man would never feel a greater pain
Than weariness of life so small and plain.

He would behold the crimson sun's first rays
And watch the limpid ripple of the fountain
Not wondering from whence the water rose
Nor who conceals the light when it is wanting
But fingering his flute where the cows graze
He would know all the grasses on the mountain
He would believe in God, be simple, quiet
And no more mysteries would contemplate.

Of one Thrasyllus it is read and written
Among the things of old Antiquity
That over many years his mind was smitten
On account of a great infirmity
And while beside himself, his reason rotten
He declared solemnly and stubbornly
That of the ships that sailed upon the seas
Those docking at Piraeus were all his.

The mighty lord in earnest he would play
Beyond the lowly carefree life he led:
He felt no loss for ships that went astray
And for those safe returning he was glad.
Not many years had gone by when one day
His brother Crito who had been abroad
Came home, and seeing how his brother sickened
His pity by fraternal love was quickened.

Giving him up to doctors, wisely kind
He makes him take the cure he cast aside
Sad that to bring him back to his right mind
He robs him of the sweet life he enjoyed!

'O brother in false colours, friend of late
Wherefore did you remove me,' he complained
'From that more peaceful life, free in all things
Which no amount of reason ever brings?

'To what king, to what duke was my knee bended?
For what great lord did I seek robes to borrow?
How much did I care if the world had ended
If nature's pattern would be changed tomorrow?
But now with grief my happy life is blended:
Now I know what is toil, and what is sorrow.
I am restored, and I will tell you this:
Folly is wise and ignorance is bliss.'

You see quite clearly here, my Lord, that such
Over all living souls is Fortune's power
Save him who does not know or feel so much
Whose innocence escapes ambition's lure.
He can mock those who blindly keep in touch
From a life uneventful and obscure
Nor will he swing forever down and up
Poised between evil dread and treacherous hope.

But if I were vouchsafed by heaven's throne
Some quiet, lowly, sweet condition where
With just my Muses I might live alone
No more demoted to a distant shore
If there I were not known to anyone
Nor knew myself any superior
Save you, who long like me to live at ease
For well I know you are not hard to please;

And suddenly those herbs with art combined
Restore him to that health long since denied
But poor Thrasyllus, now no longer cracked
Thanks Crito for the thought but not the act.

For realising he was under threat
Of toil to which by sense he was constrained
And that enjoyment of his former state
Due to delusion now was at an end

If at the brink of a pure limpid fountain
That springing up in bubbles would invite
A sweet small bird to sing for us, recounting
Who had divided it from its dear mate
And then, with snow covering the green mountain
The cold would lead us to a friendly gate
Reviving thus our spirits for sweet study —
A surer sustenance than any body;

Petrarch would sing of that illustrious
Laurel whose lady kindled his refrain
And in grand, rare style would make glorious
That crystal stream whose flow he could contain;
Sannazaro would play the flute for us
Now in the mountains, now upon the plain
And gentle Garcilaso would not plague us
With his sweet praises of the unruly Tagus

And also in our midst we would find her
Whose memory, whose bright look I have pressed
Alone into my soul, because it there
Abides in essence, pure and manifest
Through the high influence of my high star
Softening the sternness of her virtuous breast
And twining in her hair a wreath of roses
Whose radiance the jealous sun forecloses

And there, while I had garlands still to weave
Or else in winter, snug beside the fire
I would tell you of all the woes that grieve
A heart besieged by love and pure desire:

I would not then demand that Love should give
The state of poor Thrasyllus, mad and queer
But that I should have my intelligence
Doubled, and by so much increased my sense . . .

But whither is my fancy taking me?
Why do I daydream of a happy ending
If Fortune leads me so far from the way
Even towards my hopes she is unbending;
If Love gives me a new mentality
Whereby the place, the time, the false pretending
Of good make me feel so out in the cold
That daydreams are the most that I can hold?

When all is said, Fortune and Love conspired
Against me, the more grievously to bruise me:
Love saw to it that what I most desired
Was vain, only that Fortune might refuse me.
To this state time has brought me and required
That I should live therein till life should lose me
But I do not believe this can be so
For I fear that I still have far to go.

In 1803 Lord Strangford published *Poems from the Portuguese of Luis de Camoens*, the first appearance in English of a substantial selection from Camões' lyrics. By then Beckford, Byron and other English visitors and residents had established Portugal in the Romantic imagination. Among Strangford's readers was Elizabeth Barrett. She perceived parallels in Catherine's love for Camões with her own for the poet Robert Browning and wrote a long poem on the theme, from which three stanzas (of nineteen) are printed below. Browning was touched by the poem and took to calling her his 'Portuguese'. She then wrote for him those personal poems which, when he persuaded her to publish them, were released at first under the double disguise of a pseudonym and of a translation: *Sonnets from the Portuguese*. Through this title she was able to acknowledge the origin of her inspiration and to refer, perhaps, to the pet name Browning had given her.

Catarina to Camões

Dying in his absence abroad and referring to the poem in which he recorded the sweetness of her eyes

*

On the door you will not enter,
I have gazed too long – adieu!
Hope withdraws her peradventure –
Death is near me – and not you.
　　Come, O lover,
　　Close and cover
These poor eyes, you called I ween,
'Sweetest eyes, were ever seen'.

*

But all changes. At this vesper,
Cold the sun shines down the door.
If you stood there, would you whisper
'Love, I love you', as before, –
　　Death pervading
　　Now, and shading
Eyes you sang of, that yestereen,
As the sweetest ever seen!

*

O my poet, O my prophet
When you praised their sweetness so,
Did you think, in singing of it,
That it might be near to go?
　　Had you fancies
　　From their glances,
That the grave would quickly screen
'Sweetest eyes, were ever seen?'

ELIZABETH BARRETT BROWNING

Apotheosis

Title-page of the edition of *Os Lusiadas*, published in Goa, 1581.

LVIS DE CAMOENS

SPAINE gaue me noble Birth: Coimbra, Arts
LISBON, a high-plac't loue, and Courtly parts
AFFRICK, a Refuge when the Court did, frowne:
WARRE, at an Eye's expence, a faire renowne
TRAVAYLE, experience, with nee short sight
Of India, and the World; both which I write
INDIA a life, which I gaue there for Lost
On Mecons waues (a wreck and Exile) tost
To boot, this POEM, held up in one hand
Whilst with the other I swam safe to land
TASSO, a sonet, and (what's greater yit)
The honour to giue Hints to such a witt
PHILIP a Cordiall, (the ill Fortune see!)
To cure my Wants when these had new kill'd mee
My Country (Nothing — yes) Immortall Prayse
(So did I, Her) Beasts cannot browze on Bayes

THE
LUSIAD,
OR,
PORTUGALS
Hiftoricall Poem:
WRITTEN
In the PORTINGALL Language
BY
LVIS DE CAMOENS;
AND
Now newly put into ENGLISH
BY
RICHARD FANSHAW Efq;

HORAT.
Dignum laude virum Mufa vetat mori;
Carmen amat quifquis, Carmine digna facit.

LONDON,
Printed for *Humphrey Mofeley*, at the Prince's-
Arms in St *Pauls* Church-yard, M. DC. LV.

Frontispiece and Title-page of the first English translation, by Sir
Richard Fanshawe, of Camões' *Os Lusiadas*, published in London,
1655.

LUIS DE SOUSA REBELO : *Camões – Man and Monument*

I N 1572 LUÍS DE CAMÕES PUBLISHED his long awaited epic poem, *Os Lusiadas*. Dedicated to the ruling monarch, King Sebastian, the poem was immediately seen by its readers as far more than an account of the adventures and hardships endured by Vasco da Gama and his men while searching for the sea-route to India. Camões had used the voyage not just as a subject of a narrative, but as an allegory of the search for new moral values. In the structure of the poem the voyage marked the dividing line between the past and the present. The past was the story of the people of Portugal from their beginnings as a nation; the present was the reality of an empire than stretched all over the globe and demanded countless sacrifices from the Portuguese on land and at sea. By the time Camões wrote, hindsight allowed an assessment of the initial imperial experience of the Portuguese. He believed it was his duty as a poet to write an epic that would examine in a critical light the deeds of his contemporaries, interpret history, and express the doubts and fears of his generation. And it should be an epic of modern times – illuminating the transition between the old and the new, between inherited knowledge and the scientific revelations brought about by the discoveries, voicing the anxieties and frustrations of a people still thwarted by the encumbrances of the past in an age that claimed the right to self-expression and individual freedom.

These covert objectives are certainly attained in *The Lusiad*. There are lengthy surveys of Portuguese history in episodes of great poetic beauty. Told by Vasco da Gama or his brother, these accounts reveal the spirit behind the events and are in themselves an interpretation of past history. The poet intervenes frequently at critical stages of the narrative to voice his own views. In fact, Camões is present in the poem under many disguises. He is the epic narrator; his is the voice of the gods; like a novelist, he impersonates all the characters who appear in the narrative; and he appears in his own right – the poet and the soldier, who knows the rash realities of the empire and has had his share of misery and suffering. His autobiographical presence adds authority to the poem, for his own extraordinary adventures appear as a part of Portuguese history itself.

In 1572 times were perilous for Portugal. The eighteen-year-old King Sebastian showed interest only in war and religion. That was a source of great anxiety, for if he failed to produce an heir the crown would pass to a Spanish prince. Influenced by a messianic aura that had surrounded him from the day of his birth, King Sebastian believed that God had destined him to be the scourge of Islam. To conquer Mauritania and extend Portuguese power as far as Palestine: such was his dream, and to it he devoted all his energy and the nation's resources.

Camões knew the country's mood and in *The Lusiad*, availing himself of the authority of a writer, he rebukes the King for being still unmarried and for shunning the company of women. He is sympathetic to the King's plans for a crusade, yet he foresees the dangers and wants to prevent a crisis of succession. His warnings were justified by

Engraving of Camões, who was thus celebrated – along with Homer, Virgil, Dante and Milton – by William Blake. (*City of Manchester Art Gallery*.)

events. In August 1578, the young King led a large army into Morocco; in the sands of al-Ksar el-Kebir he was killed, and the best of the nobility and the army with him. On June 10, 1580, Camões died, describing Portugal as being in a state of 'vile, exhausted wretchedness'. A year later, Philip II of Spain, boasting 'I inherited it, I bought it, I conquered it', arrived in Lisbon in the wake of his armies to become King of Portugal.

Some of his biographers claimed that Camões loved Portugal so much that he had returned 'not only to die in her bosom, but with her'. The saying is apocryphal, but marks the beginning of a Camõean mythology built upon the critical, admonitory tone assumed by the poet in *The Lusiad*. Highly praised by a small minority from its first appearance in 1572, the poem soon began to gain an audience not only in Portugal but in Spain. In the remaining eight years of his life Camões could follow the success of his epic among the intellectuals and the nobility of both countries. Spain and Portugal, despite their different languages, formed a cultural community. Castilians, like King Alfonso X in the 13th Century, had composed delightful songs in Galician Portuguese and many a Portuguese poet, including Camões himself, had written poetry in Spanish. Spain was for Camões a great and respected rival in the joint plan of discovering and dividing the world between them, and his patriotism was never diminished by his admiration for Castile. For their part, Spaniards saw *The Lusiad* as their epic too. In that great 16th Century debate about whether ancient or modern ways were superior, the poem came down in favour of the modern mind. The Spaniards were receptive to his condemnation of the abuses and vices that had accompanied Portuguese aggrandisement, which were not unlike those they had shown in acquiring their own possessions. An admiration for Camões and his work helped to generate a climate of sympathy in Spain for the despair of the Portuguese. The news of King Sebastian's defeat met with no rejoicing in Spain. The cities complied with King Philip's order of recruitment with great reluctance, and his professional troops, gathering on the Portuguese border, showed no enthusiasm for the campaign. The Duke of Alba, the commander-in-chief of the invading forces, opposed the annexation and warned the King that the militia would prove more of a hindrance than a help to the regular army. As Philip's troops marched into Portugal, *The Lusiad* was admired reading at the universities of Alcala and Salamanca and elsewhere. Already by 1580 two Spanish translations had appeared, and another followed in 1591. The lyric verses of Camões, known previously only in manuscript, were published in Lisbon in 1595 and revealed him to the Iberian intelligentsia as a supreme lyric poet too.

During the period of the Spanish occupation, known as the period of the Dual Monarchy, the admiration for Camões remained unabated. The Portuguese editions of *The Lusiad* published at the time had certain passages removed or changed in order to contain anti-Castilian feeling in the country. Camões, in describing in patriotic terms the war of 1385 against Spain, showed deep respect for a valiant enemy: yet, despite the poet's fair-minded approach, the censor deemed it necessary to expunge from the text any adjectives that might hurt Spanish pride. For the Portuguese, in their hour of capitivity and tribulation, *The Lusiad* became the national Bible. Looking into the mirror of the past and learning from the judgements passed by the poet on the dangers of ambition and the perversions of power, the Portuguese took *The*

This portrait of Camões, bearing the inscription 'Fernando Gomes fez in Lx' i.e. (15)60, is reputed to have been drawn from life.

95

Engravings by Fragonard and Desenne for an edition of *Os Lusiadas* published in Paris, 1837.

Above left: The Council of the Gods. (Desenne)
Above right: Venus calms the winds and waves. (Fragonard)
Below left: Vasco da Gama at last sets foot on Indian soil, at Calicut. (Fragonard)
Below right: Camões inspired, at the grotto in Macao, named after the poet. (Desenne)

Lusiad as a book of moral guidance at a time of intense national distress. In the remote outposts of the empire, the colonial governors, the military officers, the missionaries, and many soldiers beleaguered by powerful foes (for they were now exposed to attack by all the enemies of Spain as well as by their own) found in the epic consolation for their troubles and shining examples of bravery to inspire them in the fight against their adversaries. The triumphs of the past came to have their parallels in the present. In due course, Dutch colonial ambitions were countered and destroyed in Angola, and although Indonesia was lost to the Dutch they were expelled from Brazil. During these anxious times, in many Portuguese homes, the epic became a manual of patriotism. Manuel de Faria e Sousa produced a long commentary (written in Spanish, and published in Madrid) on both *The Lusiad* and the lyric poetry of Camões. It is a sound and scholarly work in three tomes that attests to the poet's stature among his peers and his impact on cultural circles in both Portugal and Spain.

In 1635, Sir Richard Fanshawe was appointed as secretary to the British ambassador in Madrid. On his return to England he was involved in the turmoil of the Civil War. Placed under house-arrest by the Parliamentarians, he used his enforced leisure to translate *The Lusiad* into English verse. The poem was published in 1655. By then Portugal had rebelled against Spain (1640) and had re-gained a precarious independence. During the long war with Spain that followed, Portugal forged new alliances with Spain's old enemy England, and this shared hostility led to renewed treaties and finally to the marriage of Catherine of Braganza to Charles II. Thus the translation by Sir Richard Fanshawe came out at a time of a close English interest in Iberian affairs. It had only a limited success, however, being highly appreciated only by a small group of intellectuals. The lack of a wider appeal may be attributable in part to the verse form used by Fanshawe, for he wrote in Italian stanzas which had been displaced in public favour by the blank verse chosen by Milton. Milton, incidentally, seems to have known Camões' epic. In *Paradise Lost*, Books I and II, there are direct allusions to Vasco da Gama's sea-voyage to India, and in Books XI and XII Milton uses the device of the Archangel Michael taking Adam up a mount to show him a vision of the future, as in *The Lusiad* Thetys takes Vasco da Gama, and Milton adopts for his description of the physical universe a shape and order closely similar to that of Camões. Fanshawe was also impressed by Camões' lyrics. In 1697 he included translations of a sample of Camões' sonnets in his anthology of foreign poetry and these were well received.

Meanwhile, inside Portugal and Spain, many poets followed the trail blazed by Camões. Epic poems that came out at this time imitated *The Lusiad*, and the variety of themes and forms he had explored provided a flexible vehicle for the expression of individual feelings. The restoration of the Portuguese monarchy stimulated new interpretations of Camões' masterpiece. Father António Vieira, S.I. (1608-1697), the greatest Portuguese writer of the century, examined the text of the epic, looking out for secret meanings, and ingeniously traced complex patterns of words and events which he deciphered as indications of the future destiny of the country. In his *History of the Future*, written between 1664 and 1665, Vieira interpreted many passages of the poem to show the great role that Portugal would assume in the world as an independent nation. Coming across the lines in *The Lusiad* (I.24), where the poet states that, as result of Portuguese exploits, the Assyrian, Persian, Greek, and

Engraving by Fragonard for an edition of *Os Lusiadas*, published in Paris, 1837. The giant Adamastor threatens the Portuguese as they invade his domains in rounding the Cape of Good Hope.

97

The laying of the foundation stone in Camões Square, Lisbon, for the statue of the poet by the sculptor Victor Bastos, erected in 1867. (Contemporary engraving reproduced from *História do Regímen Republicans em Portugal vol i*, Lisbon 1930.)

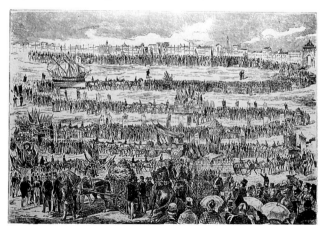

Roman empires would be forgotten, Vieira claimed that Camões intended to announce a new empire. That would be the fifth, the empire that had been predicted in the Book of Daniel. The biblical prophecy was now fulfilled. Tangible signs of the new era were the Portuguese victories over the Dutch who had for so long threatened the integrity of the Portuguese possessions overseas. In such ways does political polemic feed on poetry. In less than a century *The Lusiad* had become the epic of the modern age, a guide to the education of the Christian prince, a treatise of statecraft, the Bible of nationalism, and a prophetic book for the destiny of Portugal. The first canto of the poem was even used by small Jewish communities of Portuguese extraction as a text for messianic expectations. All these different, and often conflicting readings of Camões' epic make it one of the special cases in literary history. Like Virgil's *Aeneid*, it was regarded as a book whose author had been divinely inspired, so that *The Lusiad* – almost on a par with the scriptures – might be expected to contain esoteric meanings.

The Spanish occupation of Portugal and the restoration of the Portuguese monarchy after 1640 had the effect of drawing the world's attention to Portugal and its culture. Spain and England were now followed by others in discovering *The Lusiad*. In spite of the praise heaped on Camões by Cervantes in Spain, and Tasso in Italy, it was as late as 1658 that the first Italian version of the epic was produced. In France the first full translation of the poem did not appear until 1735. The intellectual climate created by the Enlightenment fostered a

The civic procession and other events marking the decision by parliament to celebrate Camões' birthday as Portugal's national day, July 1980. (Contemporary engravings reproduced from *História do Regímen Republicano em Portugal vol 1*, Lisbon 1930.)

new school of criticism which tried to apply the principles of formal logic to the study of poetry. *The Lusiad* was examined from a rationalist viewpoint; earlier reservations about the poem surfaced again. Previously Camões had been reproached for bringing the pagan gods into a Christian story; now his critics found such an inconsistency affected the coherence of the poem and its psychological credibility. They extended the same judgement to Camões' lyric poetry, and underlined all sorts of strange contradictions and irrational statements with a pained surprise. Their narrow view of poetic proprieties, their refusal to admit symbol and metaphor except of the most formal and obvious kind, soon led to their discredit. This was especially the case when the attempt was made to put their easy critical formulas to the test of hard practice. Epic poems inspired by new rationalist ideas, with the intent of superseding *The Lusiad*, proved to be poor imitations and ponderous failures.

In other ways the Age of Reason, particularly outside Portugal, was responsible for a sensitive and refined approach to Camões' epic poem. There was a new reading public to appeal to, interested in different cultures and literatures. The Lisbon earthquake of 1755 had struck the imagination of all Europe and made Portugal news. From Britain, for example, writers as distinguished as William Beckford and Robert Southey visited the country, reinforcing the knowledge and interest attaching to Portugal from past associations, strong trading links, and the presence of a sizeable local British community. William Julius Mickle took advantage of the mood of the public to produce a new English translation of *The Lusiad* (1771 and 1776). Highly praised for the fluency of its verse and for other poetic qualities, Mickle's translation managed to

The statue of Camões in Lisbon, draped in black, was the gathering point for patriots objecting to the ultimatum from Britain on 11th January 1890, arising from a clash of British and Portuguese expansionary claims during the 'scramble for Africa'. (*Diario de Noticias.*)

keep the spirit of the poem and yet to reflect the aims and concern of his own age. For Mickle, *The Lusiads*, or rather *The Lusiad* in his own rendering (a title which shifts the emphasis from the Portuguese themselves to their deeds) was the epic of 'commerce and free trade' – a judgement that struck a chord in many English hearts at the time. Mickle's long introduction to the poem is dedicated to the English East India Company, for which he worked. He expounds the advantages of that international trade which the Portuguese discoveries had made possible. He rejoices that, thanks to an enlightened King who had believed that the inter-dependence of trade would bring peace, the world had been explored and revealed as a commonwealth of nations happy to exchange both their goods and their cultures.

The invasion of Portugal by Napoleon's armies rekindled an interest in *The Lusiad*. The poem became once again a model and a guide for a meditation on the country's fortunes. To avoid being seized by the French, the Portuguese royal family had sailed to Brazil and set up court at Rio de Janeiro. Grave doubts had been raised about the political wisdom of this decision. But as soon as the French were forced to leave, beaten by the combined effort of the British and Portuguese armies, the general view was that the right choice had been made at the right time. *The Brasilíada* (1815), written by Thomaz Santos da Silva under the *nom de plume* of Francisco Mello e Castro, celebrates the liberation of Portugal and praises the move to Brasil in epic tones borrowed from *The Lusiad*.

The year 1803 had seen the publication in London of Lord Strangford's *Poems from the Portuguese of Luis de Camoens*. Strangford was the first secretary at the British Embassy in Lisbon and had been involved in the plans to move the Portuguese royal family to Brazil. His selection of the poet's lyric verse signals a shift of interest from *The Lusiad* to an introspective poetry better suited to the tastes of the Romantic era. One of the distinguished readers of Strangford's work was Elizabeth Barrett Browning. She found in Camões' love for his Catarina a close parallel to her love for the poet Robert Browning, and in her Sonnets from the Portuguese (1850) acknowledged in her title the source of her inspiration. (See page 90).

Lord Strangford had ventured in his volume a biography of Camões based mainly on what he could gather from the poems. The autobiographical details provided by Camões are intended to give an idealized version of real situations and comprise a myth of a poet's life, so Strangford's biography is not reliable. However, he found in both *The Lusiad* and the lyrics all the ingredients needed for telling the story of a poet whose life fitted the Romantic ideal of his age. His Camões is an adventurer and a wanderer; a great artist, unhappy in love and completely misunderstood by his contemporaries; returning from India he rescues his epic poem – the soul of Portugal – even through a shipwreck; he dies in poverty, neglected by the powers of the realm. This is the version of Camões' life that gave Byron and his circle a model for the destiny of a great poet. Some of its sentiment emerges in illustrations for a great French version of *The Lusiad* published in 1837 (see pages 96, 97). In prosaic fact, the story of Camões' life was then, and is still, full

Window, circa 1514, in the Convento do Cristo, Tomar. The carved elements in the surround reflect the Portuguese triumph over the sea and its terrors, a threatening giant – such as Camões portrayed as Adamastor – thoroughly suppressed below the cill. (*Photo: Luis Filipe Oliveira.*)

Commemoration of Camões birthday (officially, 'The Day of Portugal, of Camões, and of the Portuguese Communities') at the small town of Covilha, 10th June 1988. (*Diario de Noticias.*)

A new statue of Camões by Maria Meneres (1987) in the Avenue des Portugaises, Paris. (*Photo: Serge Gulbenkian.*)

of mysteries. The documentary proof for the date of his death is undisputed, but no one is sure about the authenticity of his mortal remains. That he was unhappy in love is clear. Certainly he died in poverty, for on his return to Portugal, he was given a small pension (not as a reward for producing *The Lusiad*, but for services as a soldier in the East) and since he had to support his mother, and given that his pension was paid irregularly, he must have faced periods of hardship. However, some have claimed, in order to complete the Romantic picture, that he was not appreciated by his contemporaries. In spite of the harsh judgements he passed on them, that is simply not true.

The expulsion of the French was followed by a struggle between the absolutists and liberals inside Portugal (1820-1834) which forced many Portuguese into exile. Some sought political asylum in France; others came to Britain. A large number of these exiles were well-educated and belonged to the middle class. Their presence contributed further to the increasing interest in Portugal and its problems. Among the Portuguese political exiles, Almeida Garrett sensed the relevance of the poet's story to the context of his own time. In his narrative poem *Camões* (1825), the poet is the symbol of the persecuted genius whose misfortunes are not unlike those experienced by the liberal exiles. They too knew in their hearts the solitude of a poet's exile, the yearning for the cities and villages left behind. They too were inspired by that true patriotism which had made Camões a severe critic of national affairs. In this way the liberal imagination appropriated the legend of Camões' life, and stimulated the growth and development of Portuguese national consciousness. In 1880, following research which had just established the date of Camões' death as 10th June 1580, a group of intellectuals urged the commemoration of the tercentenary. The Portuguese Parliament voted 10th June the national day of Portugal. Initially the Royalist authorities demurred, fearing the occasion might be used for anti-royalist propaganda, but such was the enthusiastic public response that the decision of Parliament was sanctioned by King Luis I. Camões was proclaimed the national poet. His statue, which had been erected in 1867 in one of the main squares in Lisbon, became a gathering point for public meetings, and his presumed remains were moved in civic procession from their humble resting-place to a mausoleum in the great monastery of Jerónimos (see pages 98, 99, 105).

To the English in the nineteenth century *The Lusiad* and Camões' lyric verse were a constant challenge that led to frequent translations. Mickle had his successors. The poet's biography continued to fascinate the Romantic imagination. The *Memoirs of the Life and Writings of Luis de Camões* (London, 1820) by John Adamson relied on the work done by his predecessors and offered a comprehensive view of the poet's work and his status in European literature. In 1878, John James Aubertin, an engineer by profession, who had worked on the railway line between São Paulo and Santos in Brazil, published in London *The Lusiads of Camões translated into English Verse*. His sound knowledge of Portuguese makes his version one of the most faithful to the original. To the commemorations of the tercentenary of the poet's death held in Portugal in 1880 contributions were made by British authors. A further translation of *The Lusiad*, by Richard Francis Burton, came out in London that year, and in Lisbon was published a version of the epic, rendered into English Spencerian verse, by Robert Ffrench Duff. Camões' lyric poetry was also made better known. John James Aubertin issued,

The Adamastor fountain by Julie Vaz junior (1927) on the Alto de Santa Catarina, Lisbon. (*Photo: Nicholas Sapieha.*)

in London, his *Seventy Sonnets of Camoens* (1881) and Richard Francis Burton's version of *The Lyricks* (London 1884), established Camões firmly as one of the greatest lyric poets of all time.

For the Portuguese intellectuals the commemorations of 1880 had put an official seal on the bond that existed between the poet and the resurgent nation whose spirit he embodied. That new nationalist sentiment was soon to be tested. Faced with European competition in 'the scramble for

Africa', Portugal planned to link Angola to Mozambique, claiming historical rights over the territories that stretched from east to west between the two colonies. The Portuguese penetration inland in assertion of this claim clashed with British ambitions, Cape to Cairo, north to south, and led to conflict in the Zambia region. Britain reacted against the presence of Portuguese forces in the area by suspending all negotiations with Lisbon and delivering an ultimatum on 11th January 1890. The Portuguese were stung by the *diktat* of their oldest ally and felt deeply humiliated. Anti-British feelings ran high and around the statue of Camões, covered in deep mourning, large public demonstrations were held (page 99). *The Lusiad* became daily reading, a solace for wounded national pride. Camões assumed, once again, the role of a tutelary figure endowed with saving powers, to be invoked in a moment of distress.

Under the Salazar regime, particularly during the period of the colonial wars (1961-1974), the authorities tried to draw a close parallel between the struggle of the Portuguese against pagan Islam, as described in *The Lusiad*, and the battles against the emancipation movements, deemed Communist-inspired, in the African possessions. This official reading of the epic, by giving prominence to one single aspect in the narrative and by excluding those humane values Camões so frequently upheld, reduced Camões to a writer of official Portuguese propaganda. As a consequence, when Goa was integrated into the Indian Union there followed a heated debate in the press about the local statue of Camões. Some wanted it kept as part of Goan tradition, others to pull it down as a symbol of Portuguese colonialism. Emotions ran high, and the monument suffered desecration before a more tolerant mood prevailed.

By the end of the 19th Century the work of Camões and the legend of his life, already well-known in Spain, Britain, France and Italy, spread by translations through Scandinavia, Holland, Germany, Austria, Czechoslovakia, Hungary, Poland, Russia, Romania and the United States of America. In South America, in both the Spanish and Portuguese speaking regions, his fame had long been part of the national consciousness. Brazil, sharing with Portugal a common language, shares too its admiration for Camões. Imitations and parodies of his work and references to it are as numerous in Brazil as in Portugal, showing its timeless relevance and the qualities of a poetic diction that has survived changes in literary fashion. On a popular level, Camões has passed into oral tradition and folklore. Camões with his blind eye, Camões in gaol, Camões holding the manuscript of *The Lusiad* while swimming in high seas from a shipwreck . . . these are among the most frequent scenes to be found depicted on small jugs, cups and dishes sold in village fairs and small town markets wherever Portuguese is spoken. To Portuguese workers living in Paris the statue of Camões is the natural gathering point for public demonstrations in defence of the interests of their community. Camões Square in Lisbon has become the outdoor parlour for Cape Verdean workers meeting each week to swop news from home. Camões, the prophet of renewal, the epitome of humanistic values and conscience, has become a symbol for men and women of all races throughout the world who share the Portuguese language as a common bond.

In this tomb in the great monastery of Jeronimos, made in 1880, the supposed remains of Camões now rest. (*Photo: Luis Filipe Oliveira.*)

Herman Melville spent seven years wandering in the South Seas until, in 1843 at the age of twenty-five, he took a passage home as an ordinary seaman on the man-of-war *United States*. When he came to write in *Whitejacket* a slightly fictionalized account of that voyage, he expressed his fervent admiration for 'the ever-noble matchless and unmatchable Jack Chase', master of the 'tops' on the *United States*. Perhaps it was Jack Chase's character and courage which led his mates to suffer his eccentric habit of reading Camões to them in the original, 'parts of which he knew by heart', even on the approach to port: 'for the last time, hear Camoens, boys!' From this hero (to whose memory almost fifty years later Melville dedicated his last great work, *Billy Budd*) Melville acquired his admiration for Camões. In the verses printed below, Melville apostrophizes the poet: first, at the height of his powers, g his last illness in an almshouse.

To Camões

I: (*in his prime*)

Ever restless, restless, craving rest-
The Imperfect toward Perfection pressed!
Yes, for the God demands thy best.
The world with endless beauty teems,
And thought evokes new worlds of dreams:
Hunt then the flying herds of themes!
And fan, yet fan thy fervid fire,
Until the crucible gold shall show
That fire can purge, as well as glow.
In ordered ardor, nobly strong,
Flame to the height of epic song.

II: (*on his deathbed*)

What now avails the pageant verse,
Trophies and arms with music borne?
Base is the world; and some rehearse
How noblest meet ignoble scorn.
Vain now the ardor, vain thy fire,
Delirium mere, unsound desire:
Fate's knife hath ripped thy chorded lyre.
Exhausted by the exacting lay,
Thou dost but fall a surer prey
To wile and guile ill understood;
While they who work them, fair in face,
Still keep their strength in prudent place,
And claim they worthier run life's race,
Serving high God with useful good.

HERMAN MELVILLE

End Matter

Translator's Notes

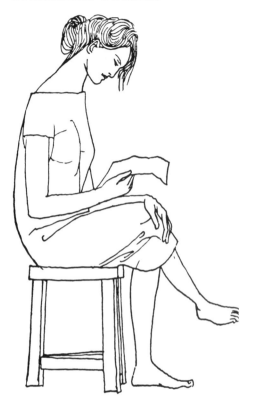

From The Lusiad

The original title is *Os Lusiadas* 'the epic of the nation of Lusus' i.e. the Portuguese. It was common Renaissance practice to refer to the epics of classical antiquity (which were Camões' models) in the plural, the singular being reserved for individual books or cantos.

page 31 THE BATTLE OF ALJUBARROTA. The Guadiana, the Douro and the Tagus (in whose estuary Lisbon stands) are the principal rivers of Portugal. At this battle some 500 English archers fought alongside their Portuguese allies against the common Castilian enemy. Two years after the victory, in 1386, the Treaty of Windsor and the marriage of John of Gaunt's daughter, Philippa, to the Portuguese king, João I, laid the foundations of the six-hundred-year-old alliance of the two countries.

page 34 FROM EQUATOR TO CAPE. In Adamastor Camões creates a new mythical figure, and by setting the giant's habitation at the Cape of Storms (not then of Good Hope) brings southern Africa into the realm of the classical gods.

page 43 EUROPE REBUKED. Cadmus slew a dragon and sowed its teeth, from which armed men sprang up. These killed one another, with the exception of five who became the ancestors of the Thebans. Having just named five European nations, the poet may be implying that a special destiny awaits them if they mend their ways.

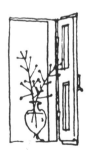

From the Lyrics and other poems

page 58   LOVE. The Spanish poet Francisco de Quevedo (1580-1645) borrows two lines and some ideas for his celebrated sonnet *Definiendo el amor* ('Defining Love'):

> It is a burning ice, a freezing fire
> It is a wound that hurts but is not felt
> It is a dreamed of good but an ill dealt
> It is a short retirement meant to tire
>
> It is being carefree with no care removed
> A coward of whom everyone is proud
> A walking solitary through the crowd
> A loving only one thing, being loved
>
> It is a liberty in jail, endured
> Till the last gasp, the final agony
> A sickness that grows worse if it is cured.
>
> Behold the boy Love, his deep mystery:
> See how with nothing friendship is
>   assured
> One who is so self-contradictory.
>
>   (tr. K.B.)

A later, very different treatment of the theme is 'The Definition of Love' by Andrew Marvell.

page 61   JACOB AND RACHEL: 'Seven long years'. See Genesis 29.

page 62   KATE: '*Kate promises the skies*'. The young poet may be using a popular song to name his 'muse', Dona Caterina de Ataíde, the royal lady-in-waiting whom he celebrates elsewhere (not in this book) under the anagram Natércia.

page 63   PARTRIDGE: '*Partridge has lost his pen*'. Ridiculing a nobleman who fell in love with a princess, a situation not unlike the poet's own.

page 65   THE REPROACH: '*False ungrateful knight*'. In the manner of a *cantiga de amigo*, the love lyric written by a man but speaking as a woman, which is perhaps Portugal's greatest contribution to medieval lyric.

page 68   DEPARTURE: 'That daybreak'. 1552: the poet, in disgrace after wounding a Court official related to Dona Caterina, leaves for India.

page 69   EXILE: 'Here in this Babylon'. Perhaps about Goa, a flourishing colony by 1553, when the poet first went there. Wordsworth could have had this sonnet in mind when he wrote 'Scorn not the Sonnet', in which he names Petrarch, Tasso, Camões ('With it Camoens soothed an exile's grief'), Dante, Spenser and Milton. Camões returns to Psalm 137 for his great paraphrase – see below.

page 71   ARABIA FELIX: 'Hard by a parched'. Probably in 1554 the poet was patrolling the Red Sea to intercept Turkish ships competing in the spice trade. The references are to Arabia Felix (in fact, Ptolemy's name for the southern, relatively fertile region), the former Greek port of Berenice in Egypt, and Cape Guardafui (now Ras Asir in Somalia) at the tip of the Horn of Africa.

page 74   THE TRANSFORMATION: 'The lover changes'. The poet attacks the notion of Platonic love, common in Renaissance poetry: if lover and beloved merge on a higher plane, what of desire? The celebration here of a real love affair suggests the Chinese woman who was Camões' great love, whom he met after being posted to Macao in 1556.

page 74   THE NEW CIRCE: 'A gentle, gracious movement'. Circe (*Odyssey* 10) changed Odysseus' men into pigs. If, as has been thought, this sonnet is about the Chinese beloved – another woman met far from home, perhaps on an island – it would explain the poet's unexpectedly positive evocation of the witch.

page 74   ON HER DEATH: 'What have I still to ask'. Apparently referring to the poet's voyage from Macao back to Goa in 1560, when he was shipwrecked off the Mekong delta, losing his beloved and his fortune, saving only the manuscript of his epic.

111

page 75 NOCTURNAL: 'The sky, the earth'. A boldly impressionistic opening leads to the fisherman poet calling in vain for the drowned beloved.

page 75 THE DREAM: 'When the long brooding'. Professionally at least, Camões called his beloved by the conventional name Dynamene ('powerful'), the only name by which we know her. Here, unconventionally, he uses the length of the name to moving effect.

page 75 TO HIS BELOVED IN HEAVEN: 'O noble soul'. Perhaps the best known of Camões' sonnets, described by Sir Richard Burton as 'the *chef d'oeuvre'*. Many translations include an English version by the great modern Portuguese poet Fernando Pessoa ('Oh gentle spirit mine that didst depart'). The sonnet is based on Petrarch's sonnet 305 (*Anima bella, da quel nodo sciolta*). A comparison vividly demonstrates Camões' contribution to Renaissance lyric:

O fair of soul, from that knot loosed and
   clear
More fair than nature ever could devise
From heaven on my dark life fix your
   mind's eyes
Lay happy thoughts aside to shed a tear.

Your heart is free of false opinion
That made your sweet look sometimes
   harsh and stern
Against me: now beyond suspicion, turn
Towards me, tune your ears to hear me
   moan.

Look at the great rock, birthplace of my
   river
And see, alone on grass the stream runs
   through
Feeding on memory and pain, your
   lover.

Where your abode was and our love was
   new
I want you to abandon it for ever
And of your friends the one who troubled
   you.

(tr K.B.)

page 76 BY THE RIVERS OF BABYLON. Camões' great Neo-Platonic paraphrase of Psalm 137 (Vulgate: Psalm 136) cast in the metre of a folk poem, like many early Christian hymns; the poet must have considered Renaissance forms too pagan. The return to Goa seems to have brought back thoughts of Babylon (see p.69). The poem's 365 lines suggest an anniversary – of the beloved's death? At least, here he renounces human love, however idealised, for the divine variety. As the poem unfolds, Babylon, at first exile, becomes this world, and Jerusalem, at first home, becomes heaven; the harps of the psalm become the instruments with which the poet went courting in his youth; the daughter of Babylon becomes the seductive flesh in which the soul is imprisoned, and her little ones to be dashed against the stones become sinful thoughts. References below are to the opening words of stanzas.

'So, seeing the ravages'. 'Harp' (as in the Hebrew and King James Bibles) renders *órgãos*, Camões' literal reading of Septuagint and Vulgate *organa* 'instruments'.

'But among my tears and sighs'. Camões quotes direct the Spanish poet Juan Boscán (1474?-1542) who introduced Italian forms into Spanish poetry.

'But, O great and glorious land'. To the English-speaking world the most familiar expression of this Platonic concept is in Wordsworth's Immortality Ode, especially section 5 ('But trailing clouds of glory do we come / From God, who is our home').

page 83 JOB'S CURSE: 'Let the day perish'. The poet quotes Job 3:3.

page 84 ON THE DISORDER OF THE WORLD. For the Renaissance the world meant human society – cf modern French *tout le monde*: Camões writes of its *desconcerto*, its lack of concert, of order, that would treat people as they deserve. The noble dedicatee was a young friend and disciple who died during

112

the poet's first spell in India (1553), so this epistle, for all its gravity, may be a comparatively early work. It embodies that curious marriage of Classical and Christian thought, typical of the Renaissance, to be found later in the epic: fate and providence cheerfully coexist. Manicheism (invoked in the name of Democritus) receives Christian rejection. Socratean serenity may lead to either indifference or cynicism, which may conceal self-interest. Ambition and even achievement are dismissed in favour of the simple life, whether deluded or not, and the poem ends with a vision of cultured leisure in good company.

'Who is there, seeing one whose virtues stood'. The 'very god of Blame' is Momus, who rebuked the smith Hephaestus for not leaving a hole in the chest of the man he had made through which the secrets of his heart could be read.

'Diogenes presumed'. Diogenes the Cynic philosopher showed his contempt for the world by living in a tub.

'And I leave other follies'. Plato the philosopher, called 'divine' during the Renaissance because of his belief in a heaven, visited Egypt, Sicily and the Greek cities of southern Italy in pursuit of knowledge.

'Why is command worth more'. This stanza was lost for 400 years, thanks to a censor who presumably objected to its fatalism. The 'Preacher' is Ecclesiastes (1:18).

'Of one Thrasyllus'. 'Thrasyllus, a man of Attica, so disordered in his mind that he believed all the ships which entered the Piraeus to be his own. He was cured by his brother, whom he reproached for depriving him of that happy illusion of mind' (Lemprière).

'Petrarch would sing'. Camões does not name him, but the allusions are clear to his world, if not to ours. Jacopo Sannazaro (c1456-1530) was the Italian author of *Arcadia*, a hugely popular pastoral romance in prose and verse. Garcilaso de la Vega (1501-36) was the first great Spanish poet of the Renaissance.

Index of First Lines

115

LUIS DE CAMÕES: *A select bibliography* compiled by Dr Luis de Sousa Rebelo

Principal translations into English.

Adamson, John. *Sonnets from the Portuguese of Luis de Camoens* Akenheads, Newcastle 1810.

Atkinson, William C. *The Lusiads* Penguin Books, Harmondsworth 1952

Aubertin, J. J. *The Lusiads* Kegan Paul, London 1878.

Aubertin, J. J. *Seventy sonnets of Camoens* Kegan Paul, London 1887

Bacon, Leonard. *The Lusiads* Society of America, New York 1950

Browne, Felicia D. *Translations from Camoens and other poets* John Murray, London 1818

Burton, Richard F. *Os Lusiadas* Bernard Quaritch, London 1880

Burton, Richard F. *Comõens: the Lyrics* Bernard Quaritch, London 1881

Duff, Robert ffrench. *The Lusiad; translated into Spencerian verse* Chatto & Windus, London 1880

Fanshaw, Richard. *The Lusiad* Humphrey Moseley, London 1665

Mickle, William J. *The Lusiad; or the discovery of India* Jackson & Lister, Oxford 1776

Mitchell, Sir T. Livingstone. *The Lusiad of Luis de Camões* T & W Boone, London 1854

Musgrave, Thomas M. *The Lusiad* John Murray, London 1826

Prestage, Edgar. *The Passion of Christ: two Elegies of Luis de Camões* Watford, 1924

Quillinan, Edward. *The Lusiad; books I-V* Edward Moxon, London, 1853

Strangford, The Lord Viscount. *Poems from the Portuguese of Luis de Camões* J. Carpenter, London 1803

Selected Criticism in English

Andrews, Norwood H., Jr. 'An Essay on Camões' Concept of the Epic. *Revista de Letras*, vol. 3, 1962, pp. 61-93.
  The Case Against Camões. A Seldom Considered Chapter From Ezra Pound's, Peter Long, New York-Paris, 1988.
Bacon, Leonard. See introduction and notes to his translation, listed above.
Bell, Aubrey F., *Luiz de Camões*, Oxford, 1923.
Bowra, C. M. 'Camões and the Epic of Portugal', *From Virgil to Milton*, London, 1945, pp. 86-138.
Giamatti, A. B. *The Earthly Paradise and the Renaissance Epic*, Princeton, 1966, pp. 210-26.
Glaser, Edward 'Manuel de Faria e Sousa and the Mythology of "Os Lusíadas" ', *Miscelânea de Estudos a Joquim de Carvalho*, Figueira da Foz, vol. 6, 1961, pp. 614-27.
Greene, T. *The Descent from Heaven: A Study in Epic Continuity*, New Haven-London, 1963, pp. 219-31.
Hart, Henry, *Luis de Camoens and the Epic of The Lusiads*, University of Oklahoma Press, Norman, 1962.
Letzring, Madonna, 'The Influence of Camöens in English Literature', *Revista Camoniana*, vol. I, 1964, pp. 158-80; vol. II, 1966, pp. 27-54. A full survey up to 1800.
Macedo, Helder Malta, *The Purpose of Praise: Past and Future in* The Lusiads *of Luís de Camões.* An inaugural Lecture in the Camöens Chair of Portuguese given on November 15, 1983, King's College, London, 1983.
Pierce, Frank, 'The Place of Mythology in *The Lusiads*', *Comparative Literature*, vol. 6, 1954, pp. 97-122.
  See introduction and notes to his edition of *Os Lusiadas*, Oxford 1973.
Pound, Ezra, 'Camöens', The Spirit of Romance, New York, London, (1st edition 1910), London, 1970, pp. 214-22.
Sena, Jorge, *'Gentle Spirit . . .'* An essay on the Camões sonnet by Jorge de Sena, in a collection of poems, translations and essays by or about Camões and Jorge de Sena. The Menard Press, London, 1980.
Walker, R. M. 'An Interpretation of the role of the supernatural in "Os Lusíadas" '; *Revista Camoniana*, vol. I, 1946, pp. 83-93.
West, S. George, 'W. J. Mickle's translation of "Os Lusíadas", *Revue de Littérature Comparée*, vol. 18, 1938, pp. 184-95.
Willis, R. C., *Camões and Kingship*, The John Rylands University Library of Manchester, Manchester, 1986.

Luís de Camões
soon counted the cost
of experience
with one eye's light lost

then sailed to explore
a new hemisphere
but he found it 'for
lack of stars less fair'

brightening meanwhile
oceans of exile
with the greatest good

whose loss cast his pen
beyond learned pain
to write it in blood.

                                    K.B.